100 CLASSIC
HOUDINI TRICKS
You Can Do

Houdini is pictured here as a young man at start of his astounding career.

by Dunninger

ARCO PUBLISHING COMPANY, INC.
219 Park Avenue South, New York, N.Y. 10003

Sketch of Dunninger by Seymour Frank

Reissued 1975 by
Arco Publishing Company, Inc.
219 Park Avenue South, New York, N. Y. 10003

Third Arco Printing, 1978

Library of Congress Catalog Card Number 74-14200
ISBN 0-668-03617-6

Printed in the United States of America

CONTENTS

Dunninger—A Biography . . . 4

Magical Memories 6

Performance Pointers 28

TRICKS

Match Magic
matchless fingers 47
light footed 79
mysterious matches 97
fire magic 98
dexterity 103
telltale match 114
balancing glass trick 128

Cigarette Stunts
weird touch 66
elusive cigarette 113

Card Conjuring
forcing a card 30
eggs-traordinary card trick 31
telltale ashes 32
the pass 34
up-in-the-air card trick 44
novel card rising effect 46
down for the count 48
houdini ace 49
20th century mind reading 51
a good turn 52
cards illusional 54
four ace miracle 58
card in hat mystery 59
color card mystery 62
elusive ace 67
second sight 68
traveling ace 71
miser's dream 84
it's in the pocket 89
magical foot 90
x-ray eyes 91
sole of the wizard 92
the mystic deck 106
the flying card 111
enchanted deck 112
phenomenal card trick 115
pocket magic 123
tipsy card trick 124
unique effect 126
cut and restored card 136
card and hat trick 138
get-together card trick 140
devil's sight 142
magical discovery 144

Money Mystifiers
vanishing a coin 36
palming a coin 37
which hand? 41
latest coin vanish 43
money flies 45
yogi coin vanish 70
banknote mystery 80
making money 82
coin in the orange 83
talking dime 105
all-seeing eye 108
the lady cries 110
penetration 129
it can be done 131
mystic jugglery 135
money talks 139

Spirit Stuff
thought reading 38
is it hypnotism? 42
ghost frame 50
spirit slates 56
pharaoh's finger 60
spirit writing 63
living or dead 64
stick magnet 69
enchanted saltshaker 74
witchcraft 75
spirited magic 86
obedient table 88
you know the number 96
seed magic 101
enchanted whistle 102
demon wine glass 107
the phone of cagliostro 116
ghostly music 120
mysterious handcuffs 122
the phantom 124
ghost in the dark 132
floating paper ball 141

Miscellaneous Magic
restored ribbon 33
enchanted handkerchief 39
patriotic billiard balls 40
chameleon bands 53
burning sugar 61
handkerchief penetration 64
jumping cigar band 72
houdini match trick 73
the plate eater 76
a sweet trick 78
columbus outdone 94
ups and downs 95
difficult catch 100
water magic 104
magnetic control 109
magical magnetism 130
color magic 133
mystic dice prediction 134
floating ball 137

dunninger–a biography

Mentalist, magician and master showman, Joseph Dunninger has mystified millions. Here's the story behind his fabulous career.

JOSEPH DUNNINGER, author of this book and the master mind whose mental wizardry and magic have baffled audiences, scientists and psychologists throughout the world, is a native New Yorker, born just before the turn of the century and reared in the heart of the city.

Dunninger's mysterious "master mind" is unique in his family. His father was a successful Bavarian textile manufacturer, and his mother performed the duties of a housewife in a purely mundane manner. Nor did his brothers have any link with the world of magic; one became a concert violinist and the other a painter and designer.

But in Joseph there was a yearning to perform magic feats at the early age of five, when he showed a marked ability at sleight-of-hand. His parents encouraged this novelty; they were much amused at his dexterity in simple palming tricks. Self-taught, Dunninger soon had a remarkable repertoire of necromancy. His childhood pastime earned him an invitation to appear before a Masonic Club at the age of seven, where he was billed as "Master Joseph Dunninger, Child Magician."

It was at this time that he caused some wonderment among his school teachers. Master Joseph did not seem to be an extra brilliant pupil, but he invariably got all his arithmetic problems correct. Could it be that he copied the answers from bright children seated near him? His seating place in the classroom was frequently changed, but still Joseph's papers were marked 100 percent.

Dunninger explains it now: "You see, I just couldn't get the wrong answer; I didn't have to work the problems out. The bright children in the classroom just sent me thought waves, and consequently I got everything right. I definitely did then and do now perform feats of genuine telepathic communication and thought reading. Of course, I have acquired a knowledge of show magic and I believe from the standpoint of showmanship I have the right to the professional license granted any entertainer to make my efforts more impressive."

By the time Dunninger was 16, he had an enviable reputation as a magician and "mentalist," a word he claims to have coined; he appeared for a year at the famous Eden Musee on 23rd Street. Dunninger outmastered many of the most prominent prestidigitators of the day, and this launched him on a vaudeville tour. It was during this tour that he developed the astounding stunt of reading the minds of members of his audiences. For many years actors had presented such an illusion through the means of code messages between an assistant in the audience and the "thought reader" on the stage. Dunninger used no assistants, and has never found it necessary to do so. In fact, he has a standing offer of $10,000 to anyone who can prove that he uses confederates or "stooges."

Dunninger headlined throughout the Keith-Orpheum Circuit, and was much in demand for private entertainment. At the age of 17 he was invited to perform at the home of Theodore Roosevelt in Oyster Bay and at the home of the inventor, Thomas A. Edison, both of whom were avid admirers of his mysticism. It was during this association that Dunninger developed some of the remarkable experiments that he uses in his performance today.

Most of the big-time vaudeville houses in the country boasted of having Dunninger on their stages in those days. Before long his "single" became a troupe of fifty with "Dunninger, the Master Mind of Mental Mystery," presenting a full evening's entertainment which included all manner of amazing illusions. Many of the acts he created have never been accomplished by another, and he is also responsible for the presence of many startling features in the repertoire of magicians currently appearing before the public.

When commercial radio started Dunninger made his air debut in a demonstration of hypnosis by radio. He was next heard in the role of a psychic detective. But neither of these features caught on. It was Daniel S. Tuthill, Dunninger's manager, who successfully evolved the Dunninger radio-formula of thought-reading. The idea quickly caught the favor of Philips Carlin, at that time vice-president of the American Broadcasting Company, and on September 12, 1943, Dunninger's first broadcast as "Dunninger, the Master Mind" was produced.

Since then Dunninger has completed two more radio series, both for Lever Brothers, over the facilities of the National Broadcasting Company network. In June 1946 he made another debut—his first nightly engagement in a hotel. For eight weeks he appeared in the Cascades Room of the Hotel Biltmore in New York City. During his stay at the Biltmore he broke attendance records that had stood for thirty-one years. He invaded television in 1948 under the sponsorship of Bigelow-Sanford carpets and for two years was one of the most popular artists on television.

Recently, Dunninger acted as technical advisor on the Paramount motion picture, *Houdini,* produced in Hollywood by George Pal. George Marshall directed the technicolor production. Tony Curtis plays the role of Harry Houdini, and Janet Leigh portrays the part of Houdini's wife, Beatrice.

Aside from directing all of the sensational effects, Dunninger trained Tony Curtis to perform many of the escapes and mystifying illusions which Houdini made famous throughout the world. All of the apparatus and tricks used in the picture were the original props which were actually used by Houdini, and were loaned to Paramount Corporation by their present owner, Dunninger.

Current Biography reports that during the war years, Dunninger assisted in three New York hospitals with the hypnotic treatment of patients; he also demonstrated and handed over to the United States Navy a device for camouflaging a warship to the point of invisibility. He refuses to explain his invention publicly on the grounds that it is both a military and a magical secret.

Mentalist, magician and master showman, Dunninger's extraordinary exploits have and will continue to bemuse layman and scientist alike. On that *we'll* bet $10,000! ★

magical memories

Houdini—Kellar—Thurston—Leon—Ching Ling Foo—these and others made magical history. Here Dunninger recalls some highlights in the lives of the men of magic.

E VERY AGE HAD its outstanding men of magic. The Pharaohs of Egypt consulted mystic wise men. The name of Cagliostro, hypnotist and man of magic, was prominent in the Middle Ages. Rasputin, 19th century self-styled holy man and politician, held sway over the court of the Czars for many years. Hitler plotted his political and military moves on the say-so of a "spiritualist" or astrologer.

Presently, men of magic are looked upon less as holy seers (a mistaken impression if there ever was one) and more as entertainers. It has been my privilege and pleasure to know a great many of the professional magicians who have been entertaining the world in my time. Their lives have been of great interest to me, and some of the stories that come to my mind in connection with these magicians will, I believe, make entertaining reading for you.

Some great names of this century were Herrmann the Great, Howard Thurston, Harry Blackstone, Horace Golden, The Great Lafayette, Ching Ling Foo, The Great Leon, Rush Ling Toy, Ziska, T. Nelson Downs, De Bierre, Cardini, Jarrow, John Scarne, Rosini—and perhaps the greatest of them all, the man to whom this book is respectfully dedicated, my esteemed friend and fellow wonder-worker, the late Harry Houdini. Further on in this book, by the way, there are 100 tricks which you can perform; many of them were of interest to Houdini—yet they are not all necessarily Houdini's brain children—they are inventions and creations which grew from seeds planted by outstanding conjurers all around the world.

But permit me to continue with the fascinating story of the history of magic as reflected in the lives of a number of great magicians.

HOUDINI

Harry Houdini had a career as full of adventurous and romantic experiences as the most imaginative novelist could possibly create.

Houdini is pictured duplicating a spiritual phenomenon as performed by Marjorie, Boston medium.

Acme

In 1936, Houdini's widow and Dr. Edward Saint conducted a "spirit test," failed to contact Houdini.

Acme

Houdini and Anna Eva Fay, who did a mental act in vaudeville, here compare notes over a crystal ball.

Houdini was born in Appleton, Wisconsin, on April 6, 1874. As a youngster he showed a keen insight into mechanics. He also had a pronounced interest in travel. In his ninth year he had a brief experience with Jack Hoefler's *Five Cent Circus* in his home town. Then came an apprenticeship as a mechanic; soon after Houdini resolved to see the great outside world with his own eager eyes.

He ran away from home as have many others who, in later years, attributed their greatness to their early contact with the corrugated side of life. He joined a small circus, and being exceptionally bright, soon learned to conduct the Punch and Judy show, to do a ventriloqual act and he also played the clown on the bars. It may be, too, that he "doubled in brass," or played in the band, though he has never said so.

Here began the experiences that later ripened Houdini into becoming the World's Handcuff King and Prison Breaker. In ex-

ploring his wits for exploits to amuse and entertain the audiences, Houdini hit upon the feat of escaping from ropes tied around him in every conceivable way. He became so expert that he eventually offered a challenge of 25 dollars to anyone who could tie him so that he could not escape. He never lost a cent.

Then came the turning point in his career when he looked for greater worlds to conquer, and began the mastery of handcuffs, leg irons, and shackles. Of course, proficiency came after a long time spent in secret practice before the public was permitted to witness the efforts of the young wizard.

After that he was a top-of-the-bill star everywhere. He made enormous salaries on the continent, where he was tremendously popular. He broke records for paid admissions all over Europe. In the week during which he performed before the Grand Duke of Russia he earned in public and private performances over $2,000, an enormous salary in those days.

After 1908 Houdini made his performance replete with new mysteries, introducing his original invention—escaping out of an air-tight galvanized iron can filled with water, after it has been locked into an iron-bound chest. He also added to this program the feat of releasing himself from a regulation strait jacket, in full view of the audience.

After touring Europe for several years, Houdini returned to America again in 1914, just before the World War.

He toured the country, appearing for two seasons at the world's largest theater, the New York Hippodrome. The first season he presented *The Vanishing Elephant*, a trick in which he caused an elephant named "Jennie" to vanish. She weighed over ten thousand pounds, and was said to be a daughter of the beloved Barnum's "Jumbo." In the second half of the Hippodrome show, he performed the *Submarine Box* feat, escaping from the same while under water.

During the war Houdini gave his services to the Government, giving performances in camps for two consecutive years. The years

INP

This photo, taken in 1914, shows Houdini shackled and in a packing case before being sealed in and thrown into a river; he made his escape within minutes. Below, Houdini at his desk in his book-cluttered office; note the marked files at the left.

INP

Two men of mystery meet: Houdini shakes hands with Conan Doyle, creator of Sherlock Holmes.

INP

Dunninger and Edgar Bergen are tickled over a feather trick the magician has just demonstrated.

Dunninger is pictured at a "spirit seance" which he conducted a number of years ago—one of many he held in successful attempts to expose fake medium stunts.

of 1918, 1920 and 1921 he became a cinema star, recognizing the fact that Dame Nature would demand her due, and that future generations might not believe that any man could perform the feats with which he was credited. So he organized a company to produce a 15-episode serial, *The Master Mystery,* in which he starred.

This was a sensational success. Later Mr. Jesse L. Lasky engaged him for a feature picture, *The Grim Game.* Before this was released, Mr. Lasky re-engaged Houdini for a second picture, entitled *Terror Island.* Both features were the sensations of the year.

Although Houdini achieved his worldwide reputation as an escape artist, magic was nearest his heart, and so in 1924 he combined his handcuff work with that of magic and illusions. For several years he toured the states with the *Houdini Mystery Show.* This continued until November 30, 1926, when Houdini met his untimely death. The great impression that his memory has created can best be emphasized by the fact that Paramount Pictures saw fit to further immortalize the Great Houdini in a recent pictured entitled *Houdini.* The writer was fortunate to have been chosen to act as technical advisor in the making of the film. To some extent I relived the days of

Houdini, in watching Houdini in the personage of Tony Curtis perform some of the sensational feats of magic exactly as Houdini performed them in bygone days. Much of the paraphernalia used in the picture was at one time the actual property of Houdini.

Houdini's Favorite Stories

Houdini could hold me spellbound for hours telling stories of magic and magicians. He particularly liked one about a certain Professor Schlamm. I remember the day he told it to me—we were sitting in Martinka's old magic shop, then located on lower Sixth Avenue in New York City. Harry turned to me with a smile and said, "Dunninger, one of the funniest experiences I ever saw happen came off back in my old museum days. There was an old-school magician on the circuit then known as Professor Schlamm.

"Now the good professor was one of those slow, patient perfectionist type of conjurers who would go to any length to make a trick perfect in its illusion. One of his pet tricks needed a fake table as a prop—and this fake table had a well in it which he could disappear things into. Schlamm loved to make metal and glass objects disappear.

"Well, one night, some practical joker

Here Harry Houdini holds $10,000 in government bonds, which he offered to any "medium" who could present a "spirit" trick he couldn't imitate.

Wide World

put a tin plate into the bottom of old Professor Schlamm's fake table just before he went on stage. As the program got under way, the prof began to disappear things into the table—and everything he dropped into the hole with a grand effect at illusion made a fine audible tinny bang on the pie plate! The old fellow was beside himself with rage, but he got through the act without blowing up.

"He never did find who put that tin plate into his table," Houdini concluded with a broad smile, but you can bet he never went on again without inspecting his table all the way through!"

Houdini also liked to tell about a magician in Germany who featured the production of livestock, such as hens, ducks and rabbits from gentlemen's coats, hats, etc. One night this magician was performing when one of the rabbits, which was to make its appearance later, got loose and dropped from the wizard's special pocket to the stage. There it sat, looking into the audience and blinking its eyes. The audience howled, but the professor—well, ala Kipling—that's another story.

The man who laughed at locks and bolts always enjoyed a joke, whether he or the other fellow was the victim. He was a good fellow always, and could laugh just as heartily at a joke on himself as at the joke on the other fellow.

Many is the laugh he had at the expense of spirit mediums. At one seance under cover of darkness, Houdini greased the secret trumpet and tambourine of the spirit medium and when the lights went on, there sat the so-called communicator with the great beyond, with hands and face well-greased and smeared.

He often told this story—while making one of his sensational escapes from an English prison, Houdini opened a cell door and confronted a prisoner who had been jailed for imbibing too freely the night before, and who wasn't quite recovered from the spree. Houdini, attired in a running suit, naturally frightened the intoxicated man, who let out a series of yells, shouting, "I'm never going to drink again! Satan is after me."

Houdini's Movie Adventure

During the filming of the *Grim Game*, in which picture Houdini jumps from one airplane to the other hundreds of feet in mid-air, the scene almost cost the master mystifier his life. No sooner had Houdini jumped from the plane, which flew about 20 feet above the other one, when the machine began to dip.

Something had gone wrong, and the top

Wide World

Photo at left shows Houdini stepping from an airtight, galvanized coffin after having been submerged in a New York pool for a record 90 minutes.

plane crashed down on the other one, which held the aviator, the leading lady and Houdini. Cameramen, actors and the director held their breath. How was it going to end? Quick-thinking cameramen continued to grind so fast that a lasting photographic record of that big moment was preserved. Thanks to the grit, quick thinking and steady nerve of the aviator, no one was injured.

"It was a *grim game,* all right," said Houdini as he helped the rescue crew untangle the aviator and the actress when the planes reached the ground.

He Takes A Dive

Houdini was an adventurous soul. He took chances few others would. There is a story told of this master of thrills that took place while he was returning from Australia. The steamer was in the shark-infested waters near Suva, in the Fiji Islands. There is a superstition in those parts that sharks, no matter how deadly and ferocious, will not attack a black man. So runs the tale and through belief in this more or less foolish fancy, native men and boys, without a thought of fear, dive deep for coins thrown into the water by tourists. Houdini stood against the deck rail with a number of other passengers and watched the antics of the native divers. Noticeable among the divers was one young native who seemed to always come up out of the water with a coin, in his mouth. All praised this man's remarkable diving ability; but Houdini, who had been watching him closely for some time, declared that the man dove into the water, grasped the coin with his hand, and then put it into his mouth. Others disputed this, but Harry finally wagered that if the diver's hands were tied behind his back, which would not interfere with his diving, that he (the diver) could not catch the coin in his mouth as he was supposed to have been doing. Furthermore, Houdini would allow himself to be handcuffed, dive off the ship and wagered he would return with the coin in his mouth.

Members of Houdini's company didn't care to have an experiment of this kind take place, but the master of magic decided that what he said was to be so. So it was. The captain warned Houdini to watch out for sharks. The native diver was called aboard and an interpreter explained what he was to do. The black diver agreed.

INP

Taken in 1925, photo shows Houdini exposing fraud of medium before a meeting of clergy; note foot.

Here Dunninger, over national telecast, reads the mind of Rep. Aime J. Forand (D.-R. I.) from a distance of 300 miles (New York to Washington, D. C.).
INP

Amazed admiration is apparent in the eyes of Marilyn Maxwell as Dunninger analyzes what's on her mind.

Houdini got into his bathing suit and brought from his stateroom a pair of handcuffs. The black fellow's hands were tied behind his back while Houdini was manacled. Two forms hit the water together, after two coins were tossed overboard. A wait of a minute and the black's head appeared. He needed air. A half minute later, feet first, Houdini made his appearance. The diver didn't have his coin, but Houdini had both the coins in his mouth. He won the bet but handed both the coins to the diver for his trouble.

Houdini And Handcuffs

One afternoon Houdini and I were visiting a theater owner of our acquaintance. Harry brought out a pair of steel handcuffs and started to toy with them. Obviously he was up to some new prank. He called in the special officer on duty at the house. As the officer entered the room, Harry made a pass at him and encircled his wrist with a handcuff. The officer was surprised for the moment, but recognizing Houdini, laughed and told the handcuff king he would not have to teach *him* the secret as to how he could release himself. Harry laughed and told him he'd call around some other day and see if he had gotten out. Suddenly the special officer, an escape artist of sorts, slipped the cuffs from his wrist and handed them to Houdini saying, "Here, open them!" Houdini took the key from his pocket and opened the cuffs.

Quick as a flash the special officer grabbed the key and the cuffs and slipped them on the escape artist's wrists, snapping them shut.

"And now that *I* have the key, let's see *you* get out of them," the officer exclaimed.

"Place the key on top of the desk," indicated Houdini, "and I'll see what I can do." The key was placed on the manager's desk in full view of all. Houdini turned around, and in a few seconds tossed the cuffs upon a typewriter desk, and then picked up the key. To the consternation and surprise of us all, the officer picked up the cuffs—they *had not been slipped from the wrists of Houdini, but had been mysteriously unlocked.*

I have time and again witnessed Houdini's escapes from the packing cases and trunks in a short space of time. I was also present at the wizard's water burial, in which he outdid a much heralded Hindu fakir who first introduced the stunt of escaping from the iron box beneath the water.

Above, Dunninger, technical advisor for "Houdini" movie, looks over the script on a Paramount set.

Nice work if you can do it—and Dunninger can. Here he ponders matters on Celeste Holm's mind.

Was Houdini ever stuck with a pair of handcuffs, was he ever fastened into any instrument of restraint from which he failed to liberate himself? This question has been asked by almost everyone who ever knew, or saw the wizard of escape in action. It can best be answered by the following sensational episode. It happened in London, England, once. The Daily Illustrated Mirror had challenged Houdini to escape from a pair of handcuffs which had been made by a Birmingham blacksmith, and which it was said had taken five years to perfect. Houdini had accepted the challenge.

A group of newspapermen brought the cuffs to the handcuff manipulator on the stage of the London Hippodrome. An audience of over four thousand people awaited the much-heralded event. Both the pressmen and Houdini asked friends to step upon the stage to form a committee to insure fair play.

Those of my readers who witnessed the work of Houdini in any of the theaters throughout the nation will undoubtly recall the speed and ease with which he would free himself from all kinds of manacles. Ten or twelve handcuffs would be locked on his arms at the same time, Houdini would kneel on the floor, and a small cabinet would be placed over him. The curtain

would be drawn so as to conceal his hands, but not his face. Usually, it would take the escape wizard about two minutes to free himself from all the irons.

But upon this night, fate had decided differently. After the lone pair of irons embraced the wrists of Houdini, he retired into his cabinet, or little ghost house, as he called it, leaving his committee anxiously awaiting results. Slowly the clock ticked on. Five minutes passed ... ten ... fifteen ... then twenty. The audience anxiously awaited results. Finally, Houdini's head peeped from out of the ghost house.

"He is free, shouted many in the audience. They were wrong. Houdini, still handcuffed, merely came out to examine the locks beneath the glare of the footlights. With saddened face, he re-entered the cabinet. Heavy perspiration trickled from his head. He seemed worried, worn and uncomfortable. He asked that a pillow be placed beneath his knees, as they were beginning to hurt. The request was granted by consent of the newspaper's representative. Twenty minutes more elapsed. The orchestra played on, and once more, Houdini emerged from the cabinet. He was still handcuffed.

Approaching his challenger, he asked that the cuffs be removed for a moment, so as to enable him to remove his coat.

Above, Dunninger (left) poses with Howard Thurston, one of the all-time greats in theater history.

At left, Thurston hypnotizes Chandra Bey during a suspended animation experiment at Ebbets Field.

INP, 1927

This the journalist refused to do, stating that he would not unlock the cuffs unless Houdini would admit defeat. He explained that Houdini had seen the cuffs locked, but had never examined them unlocked. Consequently, he thought that his reason for refusal was obvious.

Houdini became angry. He maneuvered until he succeeded in removing a penknife from his pocket. This he succeeded in opening with his teeth, and turning his coat inside out, he proceeded to cut the coat into pieces. Houdini once more entered the cabinet. Time sped on, and presently the timekeeper announced that Houdini had been in the cabinet for one full hour!

Ten minutes more of anxious waiting . . . and out came Houdini, holding the shining handcuffs in his hands. One hour and ten minutes had the wizard of escape nervously labored. The strain had been so great, and his disappointment in the length of time that he had labored so keen, that he burst into tears. Houdini did succeed, but he never forgot this episode.

HARRY KELLAR

It was New York City in the early part of the century. The theater was filling rapidly. Beautiful women attired in evening gowns escorted by faultlessly groomed men were consulting programs. Neatly uni-formed usherettes were leading late-comers to their seats. The air was filled with rare perfumes and nervous excitement. Slowly, majestically, the front curtain climbed—the house was still—and out onto the stage walked a light-footed, pleasant-faced man. A tremendous volume of applause greeted him.

Harry Kellar, dean of magicians, gracefully bowed his silent thanks to their appreciative outburst. To him this was no new thing. In this manner he was greeted upon his entrance on stages throughout the world.

Kellar—a name to be conjured with! For he earned the title of *Master of the Magic Art,* not only from enthusiastic audiences in all parts of the world, but from magicians themselves, who worshipped this genial, ever-smiling and lovable Grand Old Man of Mystery. Although Kellar toured the world several times and met with deserved success, in earlier days his career wasn't always a path of roses. His had been a hard, uphill road covered with obstacles and disappointments. Sometimes, I believe, it seemed to this master of magic that the woes and cares of the world were upon his shoulders.

(As an aside, Harry Houdini once admitted to me that Harry Kellar was his own magical inspiration.)

Dante the magician, born Harry A. Jansen in Copenhagen some 70 years ago, goes through one of his feats with his assistant, Moi-Yo Miller, who has been in his magic act for over 16 years. The trick is one in which metal rods are seen to "run through" her.

Below, Harry Blackstone and Dunninger talk over some irons; the two are friends of long standing and get together often for chats.

At bottom, a rare old photo shows Harry Kellar shaking hands with Ching Ling Foo. These magicians were famous for their feats.

Mistakes Will Happen

During the performance of the Kellar show, the feature trick was a spirit cabinet in which the magician conjured up the ghost of the famous Katy King. This was a startling illusion of the spiritualistic type, and one that thrilled millions of lovers of mystery and spirit phenomena.

The actor portraying the role of the ghost of Katy King entered the cabinet, unseen by the audience, through a trap door at the back of a large cabinet. Fixed to this door was a special lock, the key of which Fritz Bucka, as the chief assistant of the Kellar show, had in his keeping at all times. The door between performances was locked to prevent prying eyes seeking to find that which they should not see.

On this particular night of the show, Kellar dramatically worked up the spirit materialization and in his inimitable manner, announced the entrance into the cabinet of Katy King's ghostly spirit.

Once, twice, three times—the master announced the arrival of the spirit, but no spirit answered! What had happened? Kellar didn't know. Neither did any of the assistants. Passing from that with an ap-

INP

Cardini, whom Dunninger calls probably one of the finest sleight of hand artists of all time, is pictured.

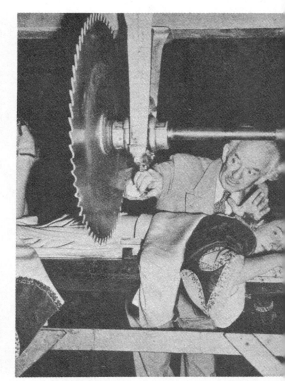

Photo by San Francisco Examiner from INP

A Blackstone specialty, sawing a woman in half, has been updated—he now uses a buzz saw.

propriate remark about the spirits holding a convention elsewhere that evening, he quickly went into another effect.

Bringing the next illusion to a fitting and sensational climax Kellar bowed gracefully to the applauding audience, but was inwardly as angry as a slapped hornet. His marvelous acting ability and showmanship concealed his real feelings from even the members of the company until the curtain fell on that act.

Kellar, who had worked himself into a frenzy, was beside himself with rage. Loudly he called for Bucka.

"What is it you want, Mr. Kellar?" asked the easy-going Fritz.

"Want!" screamed Kellar, "You're fired! You're through!"

Then he curbed his temper and continued on with the show. Between tricks he took back all that he had said in anger to Fritz.

Years rolled on. Some 23 years later, Kellar was presenting the same Katy King spirit materializing cabinet seance. It was still one of the outstanding features of his show. Perhaps this time it was a prank of the spirits—but on this night, too, the spirit of poor old Katy King couldn't make its

entrance into the cabinet. Again the door to the cabinet was locked! Fritz was busy rebuilding some stuff for the show and had forgotten to unlock the door.

This time Kellar didn't grow angry, but after the curtain went down, the master magician called his trusty assistant aside, placed his hands on Bucka's shoulders, looked him in the eye and in a pained voice said, "Fritz—I'm ashamed of you! The same mistake *twice* in *twenty-three years!*"

Tricked Tricksters

Shortly after the above episode took place, Kellar arrived in New York City and was royally entertained by members of the craft. One morning several magicians dashed into the magic shop rendezvous of Clyde Powers and each one displayed a circular announcing that at 12 o'clock that night a certain Wonder-Worker would present, at the corner of Broadway and Forty-second Streets, the master illusion of all time. A woman would be levitated into mid-air.

Soon others of the magic clan arrived, each one with a similar circular. There was excitement and comment galore. Into the store walked Kellar. Some of the wizards

Above, a close-up of Ching Ling Foo, taken at the height of his career; he had many "Chinese" imitators.

showed him the circular. His face grew purple with rage. No wonder, for the levitation mystery was his original illusion, and one that had met with sensational success wherever the master illusionist had presented it.

Three hours before the scheduled time, magic enthusiasts began to arrive. I was there, and accompanying me were Kellar, Rush Ling Toy, Leon, Caesar, Blackstone and many other mystics, all interested in this unique demonstration.

The time dragged slowly. Minutes passed into hours, and the hours seemed unusually long. More than five hundred people had gathered, many drawn by the sight of the magic crowd. Several of the more talkative magicians informed those who asked what was about to take place. Finally the hour of twelve arrived, and passed. Nothing happened. Disappointment was written all over the strained, expectant faces of the magic fans. Suddenly, someone asked, "What date is it?"

"March 31st," replied a magic fan.

"It's after midnight, and this is April 1st, isn't it?" queried the fellow.

"April fool!" yelled one of the crowd. A roar went up from the crowd. We couldn't resist laughing at the way we were all taken in by the cleverly planned hoax. The tricksters had been tricked!

CHING LING FOO

If one delves into the lives of magic men, one is sure to find, not simply a collection of stories unfolding sensational rises to success, fame and prosperity, but tales of tribulations, heartaches and of persistent battles for supremacy.

Kellar, Devant, Ching Ling Foo, Houdini, De Bierre, Blackstone and numerous others including the great Herrmann, fought for their places in the Magicians' Hall of Fame, battling obstacles that would never find their way into the paths of leaders in other vocations.

Take, for instance, the Chinese wonder-

18

Here Dunninger was attempting to determine if a six-month-old infant had a clear thinking process by mind-reading; it's evident baby has mind of its own.

Even Orson Welles got into the magic act; back in 1943 he got a show together for a tour. Here a happy soldier has just found his "vanished" ring.

worker, Ching Ling Foo. For years this master among Chinese magicians appeared only in his own country and various parts of Europe.

Later he and the troupe of 15 experienced conjurers that he headed startled American professional magicians and electrified our theater-going public from the very beginning of his appearances here.

Chinese magic, then seldom seen here, caught on at once; the clever Chinaman continued to create new effects that made this country ring with his name. Naturally there sprung up a number of "Chinese" imitators, but they were considered by booking agents as mere space fillers on a vaudeville bill.

Ching Ling Foo's specialty was producing from empty, beautifully painted and embroidered shawls various-sized glass bowls containing live goldfish. After convincing his spectators that he had nothing concealed about his person, Foo would turn a complete somersault and immediately thereafter produce a large bowl containing water and goldfish. This effect alone used to bring forth great applause. The bowl and contents weighed 90 pounds!

But soon Foo longed for the rice fields of his Flowering Kingdom, and the plaudits of his audiences began to hold little charm. Ching Ling Foo, with his company, returned then to his homeland, carrying with him untold wealth. But as he once explained to his friend Harry Kellar, he was

not unappreciative of the manner in which the American theater-goers welcomed him.

CHUNG LING SOO

About this time in England, another "Chinese" conjurer made his debut. Immediately this mysterious newcomer, known under the stage *nom de plume* of Chung Ling Soo, began to outshine the original Ching Ling Foo. For some time, even in magic circles, there was much speculation as to just who the mysterious Chung Ling Soo actually was.

Time went on and English theater-goers showered this "superior" magician from the Flowery Kingdom with applause and English coins. Gradually it leaked out that the Chinaman who was startling England was an American, well versed in the art of make-up. Chung Ling Soo was none other than William G. Robinson, a clever illusionist and character actor from Yankeeland. Soo's getup and the make-up of his assistants were perfection. Robinson even went so far as to allow himself to be interviewed, through an interpreter, by members of the British Press. His London home was fitted up in true Oriental manner with hanging lamps, rich Chinese tapestries, and whenever the gentlemen of the press were visiting him, the pseudo-Chinaman received them in this intriguing Poppyland setting.

A humorous tale is related of Chung Ling Soo in which he was being inter-

Dunninger shakes hands with former president Hoover at a recent dinner in New York City, at which time Dunninger actually read his mind.

Below, mentalist Dunninger has just startled Baccaloni, Met singer, by reading music in his mind.

Al Smith, one-time Democratic presidential aspirant, was one of millions astounded by Dunninger's talent. The photo was taken in Mr. Smith's office.

Jack Gwynne amazes an airlines stewardess by floating Helen Gwynne in air at Chicago airport.
Acme Photo

viewed by several reporters. "Do you like this country?" asked one of the scribes.

The real Chinese interpreter, who was an acrobat and trusted assistant of Soo's made answer, "I do. They are kind, generous and know as much as I do of my magic art."

"Have you ever been to America?" queried the other representative of the Fourth Estate.

"No," the interpreter translated, "but in my dreams I see large buildings and much water. And standing in the Bay I see a large statue with one hand upraised holding the torch of light, lighting the way to freedom."

"Do you expect to return to America?" asked the skeptical newspaperman.

"How can one return to a place one has never seen?" fenced the inimitable Billy Robinson, through the interpreter.

Several times during the engagement in England, Soo was invited by wealthy Chinese residents to attend social functions. Knowing full well what the outcome of accepting any of these invitations would be, Soo refused with the excuse of pressing engagements.

However, the *original* Ching Ling Foo soon began to tire of the life of a Chinese country squire. The lure of the footlights again began to assert itself. Then reports came to him of another who not only adopted a portion of his name but who was astounding audiences with many of his feature tricks.

Oriental brains began working. Foo issued a challenge to Soo. In 1905 during the month of January, Soo took up the "hat in the ring" edict and presented himself in the offices of an English newspaper to meet

Sherms, a Bridgeport, Connecticut, magician, releases assistant from cabinet which has just been punctured with numberless swords; scene was a magician's convention in Washington, D. C., 1948.

Upper right, Faye Emerson smiles with amusement and amazement at Dunninger's mind-reading.

Right, Dunninger talks things over with New York Governor Tom Dewey. He successfully read Dewey's mind; the governor was thinking "When will the legislature adjourn?" and "Will Dunninger do my radio broadcast for me tonight?" Amazing?

and outskill the skilled Foo. Robinson, alias Chung Ling Soo, had no alternative. For an hour or more he entertained the news clan with magical tricks, awaiting the arrival of Ching Ling Foo, but the fates and the keen Oriental mind decided differently.

On the following day the newspaper office received a letter from the original Ching Ling Foo, announcing that he (Foo) would meet and take up the challenge with Soo only upon the condition that Chung Ling Soo appear before the Chinese Consul in London, and prove his claim to being a real Chinaman. This naturally never took place and was soon forgotten by the readers of the papers. They had seen Soo and voted him the cleverest of Chinese wonder workers and that was enough.

Billy Robinson was a good friend of all

who worked with him. He was an ingenious inventor and a skilled magician. He was a makeup artist of remarkable ability and an actor to his fingertips. I still have and value very highly a fishing pole trick he presented me with while I was in England. This was one of the two tricks that won him great fame.

The other was the illusion he created when he would allow several soldiers to fire rifles at him; he would then catch a marked bullet between his teeth. This trick startled all who witnessed it and finally was the cause of his death. One day, through some carelessness on the part of one of his assistants, a real bullet was included with the fakes. That night, standing bravely before the firing squad, Billy smiled in his inimitable way as the rifles were fired. Robinson swayed a moment

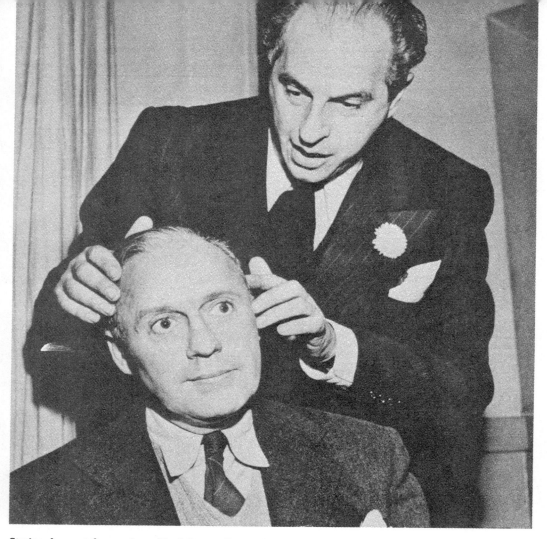

Staring down at the cranium of Jack Benny, Dunninger concentrates on Benny's thoughts. Could it be 39?

The master mentalist entertains a red-headed friend on radio show, incidentally entertaining millions.

Frank Sinatra's thoughts are apparently sweeping toward Dunninger, judging by the back curtain.

and then collapsed dead to the stage, a bullet in his skull. The curtain was rung down for the last time on the inimitable Chung Ling Soo.

THE GREAT LEON

An insurance policy sale of $25,000 would bring exclamations of delight from any live-wire insurance agent; yet a charming young lady, aged 25, who never knew a sick day in her life was refused a policy for that amount. Why?

Because, as the assistant of a magical entertainer, she was fired two and three times a day from the muzzle of a large cannon, *through a steel plate,* into a net. The illusion, one of the most sensational to be performed upon any stage, was owned and presented by the Great Leon, a magician and illusionist of considerable renown.

The effect of the illusion follows: a smiling young miss is placed in a loaded cannon. A large sheet of examined steel is mounted in a frame directly in front of the muzzle. The cannon is fired; the report is extremely loud. The projectile is seen to penetrate the plate and pass entirely through. The young lady is assisted from the net in which she lands and the steel plate is freely shown to the spectators and found to be quite intact.

Spirit mediums have time and again claimed that it is a form of spirit disintegration and materialization—in other words, that the body is transported by supernatural means from the cannon into the net through the steel plate. As a matter of fact, it was simply a fine stage illusion—accomplished by natural means. It required many years of scientific research, planning and working of several master magical mechanicians to perfect this startling and convincing magical feature presentation.

During the experimentation period, several who were tried out as assistants were injured. Advertisements were inserted in newspapers requesting the services of trustworthy assistants, with the bait of bonuses for the right parties. Quite a number applied, but when Leon or his mechanicians explained what the duties of the assistant would be, all seemed to remember engagements elsewhere.

As there was no one forthcoming, and as Leon knew whoever did act the part of the human projectile would be endangering his life, he took the duties of assistant upon himself. One day things went wrong, the Goddess of Luck winked a wicked eye, and the Great Leon woke up in New York City's French Hospital.

Things were finally straightened out by a well-known mechanician. For some weeks the illusion was presented before large audiences in the leading big-time vaudeville theaters of the country; but bad luck was to have its fling once more.

One evening an assistant loaded the cannon with a supply of gunpowder without checking with the man who was assigned to this task. The official loader charged the cannon with another supply of gunpowder. When the gun was touched off the lady in the steel shell escaped injury by some miraculous chance, but the scenery was shot to pieces and a fire was averted only through the quick work of several of the actors on the bill.

More experiments followed. The cannon was rebuilt. After two years passed by, constant experimentation brought its reward. The act was perfected and made harmless to the assistant who acted the role of projectile. After that it became a stage sensation and was shown in the better theaters throughout the nation for years.

In Palais de Chaillot, Paris, Tahra Bey lies in an imposed trance on spikes as observer jumps on him.
Acme Photo

On a set in Hollywood, Dunninger shows Tony Curtis a trick as Jerry Lewis, Janet Leigh look on.

23

Blackstone is one of the great stage illusionists now performing; here he explains a trick to retinue.

Spirit experiment in 1928 is the scene; Dunninger duplicated "spiritual" phenomena scientifically.

Usually recognizable only by voice are Amos and Andy, seen sending "thoughts" to Dunninger.

Dunninger worked in hospitals during WW II, also invented a camouflage; below, with June Havoc.

Another illusion the Great Leon has been associated with is the Fire and Water sensation. In this illusion a lady is presumably burned at the stake, a shot is fired and she makes her appearance in a glass case filled with water. She steps out of this case dripping wet. Even with this illusion several mishaps took place in various theaters where Leon was appearing. One night the lady didn't make her getaway quickly enough from beneath her shroud-like robe, and the flames shot up and severely burned her. One or two other assistants received second and third degree burns when attempting this startling effect. Leon soon perfected this illusion and danger to the assistants was completely eliminated. This too became a magical masterpiece and played the "big-time" for a long period.

HARRY BLACKSTONE

Harry Blackstone, professionally known as Blackstone the Magician, might well be called the most colorful and sensational illusionist of our time. Blackstone's success can best be attributed to his originality and spectacular presentation; also, he is one of the best sleight-of-hand artists of our day.

Blackstone presents an extremely spectacular and well balanced full evening's program of higher type illusion effects, the larger percentage of which is entirely different and much more sensational than the illusions of some of his predecessors.

He features the Karnack Levitation, an illusion in which a young lady is levitated in mid-air, high above the level of the stage, without any visible means of support. Magicians as far back as Robert Houdin have presented levitations. This effect, too, was a high point in the Harry Kellar show, but the Blackstone Levitation is a highly improved version and covers an investment of $20,000 or more before absolute perfection was developed.

Among other effects, Blackstone has discarded the now antiquated box for sawing a woman in half. He now uses a large motor-driven buzz-saw and a table instead of the old hand saw. In everything Blackstone presents, he seeks perfection and obtains it. He carries two carloads of props and about 40 assistants to make this brilliant magic show one of the outstanding spectacles of the American theater.

The author and Harry Blackstone have been intimate friends for many years. Our get-togethers can be numbered by the hundreds, yet never have I been with Blackstone when he failed to carry an array of pocket tricks which he would always pull forth and begin to demonstrate at the slightest provocation. He would play to a newsboy on the corner, a waiter in a Chinese restaurant, his barber, or even a taxi-driver as enthusiastically as he would play to an audience of thousands. This desire to do tricks is basically the secret of his overwhelming success.

Blackstone is not loved and respected merely by the hundreds of thousands who have witnessed his shows through the years, but is highly honored and respected by all outstanding members of the profession as well.

Blackstone's Boner

I once asked Blackstone what he considered to be the outstanding mishap in his career. He related the following story:

"This happened some years ago when I was appearing at the Gary Theatre in San Francisco. Several days previous to my show I had invested in a Chinese lottery ticket which I purchased from Chang, an art dealer whom I knew fairly well in Frisco Chinatown. This night as I came to the stage door, my friend Chang, with a broad smile informed me that I had won $161, which he triumphantly waved in his outstretched hand.

"Thanking him and playfully remarking that being a magician, I could easily pick a winner, I hurriedly put the winnings in my pocket and rushed into the theater. I was quite late and it was a few moments to curtain time.

"I quickly got into my dress clothes, but did not change my trousers as I was already wearing my dress trousers. That night on stage, I went through my usual routine which included 'lifting' a man's wallet without his knowing it. This fellow was one of many invited skeptics chosen from the audience to assist me in various tricks. As this man was dismissed, I called to him,

returned his wallet and said, 'Here's a little gift for you.'

"It was long after the performance that night that I missed the $161 which Chang had given me. It had disappeared. I then recalled my wallet trick—the unknown spectator was $161 richer than he was when he entered the theater! When I returned his wallet, my money, which had been in the same pocket, accidentally went with it. I often wonder what that man must have thought when he discovered that his money had multiplied— I'll probably never know!"

DUNNINGER'S CLOSE ESCAPES

Tricksters who constantly toy with fate sometimes find that fate has a way of reversing the game. In my many years on the stage as a professional magician, mentalist and escape artist, I have had a number of humorous and not-so-humorous brushes with Lady Luck. A humorous episode had to do with handcuffs that were escape-proof—a serious episode had to do with a few minutes spent inside a locked safe that almost ended in my death.

Handcuff Humor

Many years ago I carried a heavy show. My magic show consisted of 35 assistants, sometimes more. I combined self-liberation with illusions, and also employed my customary mind-reading exhibition.

One night I issued my standard challenge to any police officers to bring their own handcuffs, from which I promised I would release myself upon the stage. As I spoke, I noticed a man seated in the front row dropping buckshot into the locks of his pair of handcuffs. It is impossible for anyone to free himself from handcuffs that have been doctored with buckshot. Saying nothing I invited a committee to come to the stage to examine the cuffs and assist in manacling me. Up stepped the joker carrying his handcuffs. Watching my chance, I took the handcuffs from him and grasping his wrist, snapped a cuff onto *his* wrist, pressing the side catch.

Then I said, "I want to have the ladies and gentlemen out there see how easy it is to open those cuffs of yours with the key!"

Imagine what my predicament would have been if I hadn't by sheer luck glanced in his direction when I first made my entrance. I know from personal experience that the only way to get out of this type of handcuff is to file them off the wrists. My assistants later accommodated the embarrassed gentleman.

Gary Cooper seems shaken at Dunninger's mind-reading ability; photo was taken at NBC studio.

Even maharajas like to get in the act; here, Maharaja of Jodhpur performs his fire-from-water trick.

Not So Safe

When the magician least expects it drama creeps into his work. I will never forget the thrill and fright I received one night. Even my own assistants didn't know at the time what a narrow escape I had from being suffocated to death.

It came about in this manner—I used to feature a strait jacket release, and an escape from a large safe. The safe was always borrowed from the leading safe dealer in whichever town I happened to be playing. One night I would perform the safe escape, and the next evening the strait jacket release.

This night I stepped out on the stage and announced I would endeavor to make my escape from the safe. In this trick I secretly used a flashlight, so as to see in the darkness of the safe in order to operate the tumblers from within. It perhaps isn't generally known, but tumblers in a safe can be operated from the inside by anyone understanding their workings, by removing a covering plate after taking out the screws which hold it in place.

On the heels of my announcement a voice in the audience rang out, "I demand that you, Dunninger, escape or make an attempt to escape from this strait jacket!"

"But my dear sir, tonight I have scheduled my escape from this safe," I announced to the challenger as I pointed to the large safe which stood on the big stage.

"Makes no difference. I insist on the strait jacket!" called the man in the audience.

"If you insist, sir, I shall leave the decision to the audience, whom I am here to please." I expected the audience to pass his challenge up, but they yelled that I should do both the strait jacket escape and the safe release, so I was forced to comply.

I requested the challenger to step upon the stage with his restraint jacket—it was the type used only on the most violently insane unfortunates. Removing my coat, in the pockets of which were my small trusty screwdriver and flashlight, I tossed it over a chair. During the process of being manhandled and buckled into the restraint apparatus, I forgot all about it.

Officers recruited from the audience who assisted in the operations were experts in their line. I was handled none too gently, and the spectators out front seemed to sense this, for hisses greeted the efforts of the strong arms.

When I was bound in approved asylum style I requested the committeemen to stand to one side. In full view I managed to make my escape from that murderous restraint jacket. A thunderous volume of applause greeted my release and for a few moments I stood, nearly exhausted, bowing my thanks to the audience for their generous applause.

Dr. Zina Bennett, an official of the International Brotherhood of Magicians, chats with Blackstone.

Henry Kaiser, famous American industrialist, finds Dunninger's mental feats amazing and amusing.

Dunninger's radio show and, later, his TV show, were heard and seen by millions of faithful fans.

When I had regained my breath, I was ready to try the safe trick. The safe was opened, I stepped into it, and it was quickly locked. I knew my assistants were wheeling my cabinet around the safe to cover my escape methods from prying eyes. I was ready to work. I started to place my hands in my coat pockets. *Then I remembered. My coat was outside on a chair—and I had neither screwdriver nor flashlight!* Here I was in total darkness, with barely enough room to move, and without the necessary means to escape!

Fumbling as best I could with the plates over the tumblers—with the oxygen being used up—with no means of attracting or signaling my assistants—I was gradually enveloped in panic! Beads of perspiration dripped from my forehead striking my cold, nervous hands like drops of melted lead—I fought the panic at my throat.

Fearfully searching my pockets for anything which could be used as a tool, I came across my key ring! The gods were with me, for on this key ring I had a skeleton key with filed edges. In my panic I had nearly forgotten it.

Now I set to work with the key on the plate covering the tumblers. My head seemed ready to burst—my tongue was parched—my head splitting—I tore the collar from my dress shirt—then the neck—I must continue to breathe—finally the tumblers clicked into place—I was free—free!

I had just enough strength left to push open that door—the sounds of the orchestra sounded faintly in my ears—I staggered forward—fell—then darkness!

When I came to, I was seated in a chair backstage. A doctor was holding a bottle of smelling salts to my nostrils. My assistants and the stage crew were standing about, faces as white as sheets.

"Narrow escape, that!" volunteered the physician.

"Dunninger, we were afraid you were gone!" my first assistant told me.

"The lamp and the screwdriver were in my coat—" I was too weak to talk.

"Yes. I found that out after they had locked you in," replied my assistant.

"That safe stuff is out from now on!" I managed to say. Then I heard my man, who had been with me for several years reply, "Amen!"

Never again, in the many years I continued to do escape stunts, did I include the safe escape. ★

Dunninger puzzles Quentin Reynolds with a variation on the Devil's Sight trick, illustrated on page 142.

performance pointers

Practice, patience and props are invaluable to the tyro magician.

Dunninger here explains the how, why and where of the magic art.

ANTIQUATED BOOKS on magic are in agreement, as are most of our modern publications, in setting forth a series of rules of performance important to magicians both professional and amateur.

These rules have stood the test of time and are as important today as they were when they first appeared in print, as far back as the thirteenth century. Briefly they are as follows:

• Never repeat a trick for the same audience. An unsuspecting audience not knowing the substance of the trick the conjurer is about to perform, cannot ordinarily follow the procedure leading to the climax of the effect. The audience is therefore unable to discover the *modus operandi*, or method of operation. Should you foolishly repeat the trick, spectators, now familiar with the climax, will study your moves and presentation more closely. The danger of discovery is therefore obvious.

• It is important that the conjurer stand before a mirror and observe carefully all of his manipulations. In this way he observes what the spectators see. This method of obtaining near perfection in sleight of hand manipulation is essential.

• A fine silk thread is a magician's best friend. A trifle exaggerated perhaps but technically important. It may be well to add that a long black human hair is equally as important, and of greater invisibility at closer range, than would be the thinnest of silk thread.

• A sticky substance used as a temporary adhesive for cards, coins and the like is essential. Many substances will do, and these are mentioned in the appropriate tricks that follow this chapter.

• We have found that the best make of playing cards for magical purposes are those of cheaper quality, strange as it may seem. Steamboat cards or Bee's are excellent for sleight of hand purpose. The better grades are usually of heavier texture and have a polished surface which gives them a tendency of being slippery and harder to handle.

• For coin magic it is well for the student to get a supply of specially made palming coins, available at the better magic shops. They are of half-dollar size and sound identical to a genuine fifty cent piece. They are thinner than Uncle Sam's half dollar and are easier to handle. They also have a deeply beveled edge which is a great aid to magicians for palming. These are available for about a dollar a dozen.

• In our opinion, the most essential rule in magic is to properly cultivate misdirection. Briefly it consists of the magician's ability to direct the attention of the audience away from the sleights and numerous points of deception exercised in every magical performance. This can be done by developing a professional ability to perform feats of magic and illusions in a nonchalant manner. Always look away from the things an audience is not supposed to see.

Where To Buy Equipment

Manufacturers of magic apparatus are numerous. There are literally thousands of trick shops throughout the nation. Unfortunately the greater number of these cater mostly to pocket novelties, tourist souvenirs, post cards and varied merchandise other than magic.

My editor has therefore advised me to come to the aid of the party and supply constructive information as to where suitable and reliable apparatus might be obtained.

The Magic Center, 739 8th Avenue, New York City. Many present-day magicians have secured their apparatus from this concern, which caters to both professional and amateur magicians. They have a catalog which they will forward to anyone sending 75 cents and asking for it.

Perhaps the oldest supply house of magical equipment in the world is the Hornmann Magic Co., 304 West 34th Street, New York City. It was established in 1856 and was from time to time owned by prominent magicians, including Harry Houdini. This concern also distributes an illustrated catalog describing the effects they handle and listing the price of each one. The catalog will be mailed to you for 50 cents per copy.

Another magic shop of interest is Louis Tannen, Inc., 1540 Broadway, New York City. This store supplies stage tricks, illusions, magic sets, magic books, and all kinds of equipment to beginners, amateurs, and professionals. They have a catalog which they will send to you for two dollars plus 50 cents for postage and handling.

Another outfit, although it is a wholesaler only, is D. Robbins and Co., Inc., 127 West 17th Street, New York City. They are distributors of magic tricks and jokes to stores and jobbers. They also have a catalog, but it should be reiterated that Robbins is a wholesaler.

The tricks presented on the following pages can be, for the most part, performed with no special equipment. For the tricks which require special equipment, we recommend that you contact your local dealer in magic effects or any of the dealers mentioned above. For the readers who intend to proceed to grander and greater effects, and who may be preparing an evening's program and would like advice, we suggest you correspond with the manufacturers named, secure their catalogs, and study them carefully. Any of the manufacturers will gladly aid you in preparing a program suitable to your needs.

The 100 tricks on the following pages were selected from among many hundreds especially for this book. None require professional ability, although some require a bit of practice before they can be presented with the desired nonchalant air of assurance. You'll find real fun in performing these for family and friends—and if you have the required ability, ambition and a flair for histrionics, who knows but that you may become a future Houdini! ★

forcing a card

Which card would you pick?
This trick is psychological.

ONE OF THE standard and most important principles in card magic is that of *forcing a card,* which is simply the trick of leading a spectator to believe that he freely selects a card from an unprepared deck. In reality, he is selecting the card *you* want him to choose.

The simplest and most practical method of accomplishing this feat is as follows: shuffle the deck or request a spectator to do so. When the deck is returned, casually cut the deck several times, holding the cards face up as you do so. Secretly note the number and suit of the top card, which is the one you are about to force.

As you approach a spectator, requesting him to select a card, divide the deck secretly in half, bringing the lower half to rest on top of the other. This action naturally brings the memorized card to the center of the deck. By inserting the first joint of your little finger into the deck directly above this card, you are aware of its position in the deck. Spreading the cards out fanwise with the request that the spectator freely choose a card, slide the cards casually from one hand to the other until you come to the one you have planted. With the thumb of your right hand, push this card forward slightly toward the spectator, at the same time slowing up the fanning of the cards.

When properly presented this type of force should prove infallible. However, should the student occasionally fail, we recommend two things. The most obvious thing: more practice. The second expedient is arming yourself with what is known professionally as a forcing deck. This is a deck with 52 cards, 51 of them being identical—the differing card is used for the bottom of the deck. These cards are also available in two or three suits to the deck; this would mean the performer could force two or three cards from one deck if required. These special decks are available at magic supply houses; with one, the performer risks no chance of failure. ★

In preparation for this trick, the name of a card is brushed onto an egg with a solution of vinegar and alum. After the egg is hardboiled, trick is "ready."

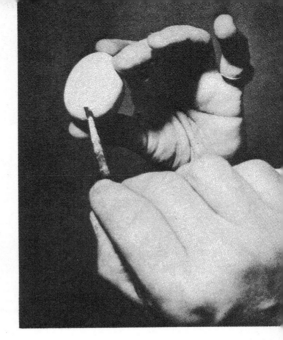

A CARD IS chosen and shuffled back into the pack. A hard-boiled egg, previously inspected, is shelled by the spectator, and the name of the chosen card is discovered written on the egg.

Method: Prepare by dissolving a little alum in vinegar (proportion one ounce of alum to one pint of vinegar). Apply this solution to the egg-shell by printing the name of the force-card. When quite dry, and no sign of writing remains, boil the egg for about twelve or fifteen minutes and it is "ready to serve." The boiled egg and the idea will keep, and can be served "fresh" when required. ★

eggs-traordinary card trick

Card is forced (see page 30) then identified when egg is cracked; initials are on egg!

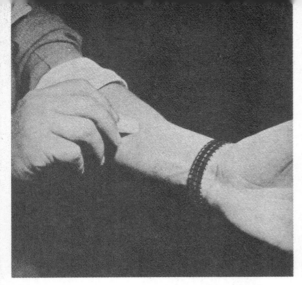

The edge of a piece of soap is used to letter AH on the arm before the trick is performed, then (upper right) the magician secretly places his selected card on the bottom of the deck. Cards are cut, piece of paper is put between halves; it is said by magician that when ashes of paper is rubbed on arm, name of card above paper will appear (below).

telltale ashes

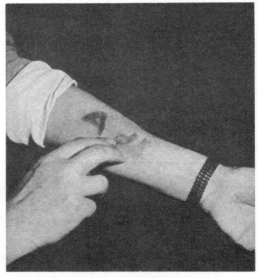

IN THIS TRICK, *the performer utilizes another method of forcing a card not previously explained, and which can be used in other tricks.* He lets a spectator cut a pack of cards and between the two portions he places a slip of paper. Then the *spectator* notes the card above the slip of paper and writes its name on the sheet. The paper is then burned, and the performer rubs the ashes on the back of his hand. The name of the chosen card appears there, in black letters.

The trick is accomplished like this. First of all, obtain a small piece of soap, and mark the name of the card on the arm, using the edge of the soap. Write K D if the card is the king of diamonds; or 6 H for the six of hearts, etc., using whatever card you may desire.

Before performing the trick, pick up the pack, and place the required card on the bottom. When the spectator cuts the pack, so that the two portions are side by side, calmly place the slip of paper on the top portion, and complete the cut. Thus the card above the paper is the required card. When the name is written and the paper burned, the rubbing of the ashes on the back of the hand will cause the invisible letters to appear. ★

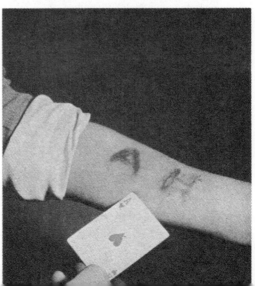

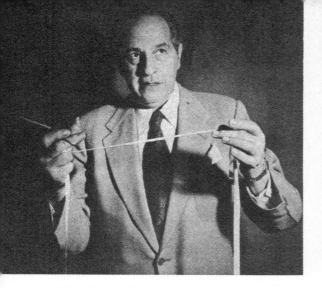

A length of ribbon is displayed and found intact.

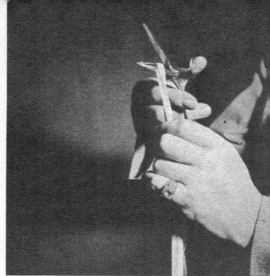

The performer of the trick cuts ribbon with scissors.

Above, the cut ribbon is displayed; ends tied.

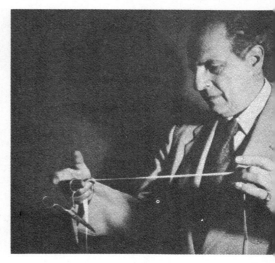

Above, mysteriously the magician restores ribbon.

restored ribbon

Below, the secret: duplicate small ribbon is one cut.

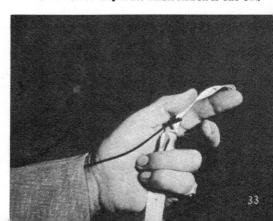

IN THIS MYSTIFYING effect a cut ribbon is mysteriously made whole again. The ribbon, after having been measured, is cut in half, a knot is made and by passing the hand over the cut portions, the ribbon again repairs itself.

The secret lies in the fact that another *duplicate* ribbon (a small loop of ribbon) attached to a rubber band is the one actually cut. When this duplicate ribbon is tied, the performer places his hand over the knot and manipulating it, secretly releases it, permitting the elastic band to draw the small piece up his coat sleeve. ★

The problem is to apparently return a card to the center of the deck, yet actually bring it to the top, where the magician can make use of it in a trick. This pass can be adapted to use in many magical tricks.

the pass

THIS IS A most useful card sleight for bringing to the top (or occasionally, to the bottom) of the pack a chosen card. It is a sleight necessitating considerable practice to achieve perfection.

A chosen card is returned to the pack. The performer, with one half of the pack held forward in the left hand, has the card placed on top. The cards in right hand are apparently placed on those in left, but are actually *slipped under them*. This is the pass. The chosen card is thus conveniently left on the top of the pack.

The method of holding the cards: those in the left hand are held with the thumb at one side near the top with the second, third and little fingers at the other. The first finger is bent so that the finger-tip is resting against the face of the cards (the hand is held palm upward). This is a perfectly natural way to hold the cards for the return of the chosen card.

The cards in the right hand, which is held to the right of, and above, those in the left, are held by the thumb at the lower end, with the second and third fingers at the top end, the cards facing downward. This is also a natural hold.

As the two hands come together cards in the left are tilted by the first finger pressing upward and the thumb downward, the lower end of cards coming under the grip of the ball of the thumb. The cards in the right hand are swiveled by the third finger pulling upward (the second finger and the thumb remain rigid).

The right hand cards are slipped under those in the left, then the whole pack is allowed to lie flat on the left hand. Though this may read somewhat complicated, the illustrations will help clarify the method. ★

1: This movement is done fast, requires practice.

2: The hands are kept in natural holding position.

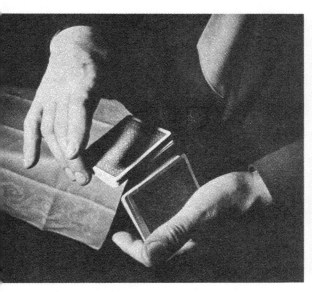

3: Performer does not keep his eyes on the cards.

4: Cards in right hand are supposedly going on top.

5: Pass is almost completed; note natural position.

6: When properly done, the pass goes unobserved.

vanishing a coin

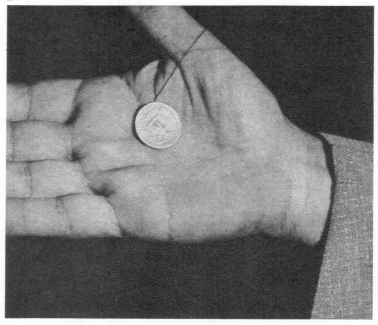

String was used in these photographs instead of thread or hair, to aid reader.

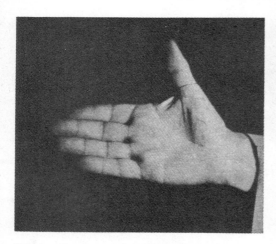

A flip, and coin vanishes! Wax, thread are used.

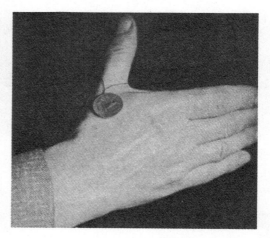

Two coins may be made to vanish at once.

PERHAPS THE MOST sought after coin effect is that of vanishing a coin. This is a necessary effect, as so many coin tricks are basically dependent upon it.

The following is simple, and easy to perform: Encircle the thumb with a human hair loop (or thread) that will reach to the center of the back of the hand, and place a pellet of wax (secreted under the thumbnail) on the knot. You now borrow a coin and secretly press the wax against one side. Pretending to rub the coin with the other hand you actually drop the coin behind the hand and now show both hands empty. By reversing the action the coin can be made to reappear. By employing both sides of the wax, two coins can be made to vanish, one after the other or both at the same time. As in other tricks, practice before you perform. ★

palming a coin

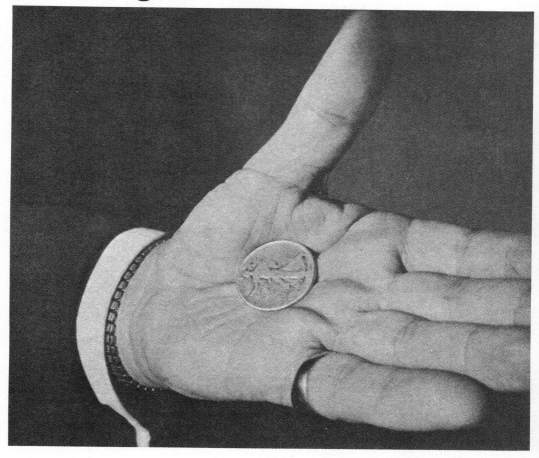

It takes practice to learn this properly, but it's worth it, since so many other tricks depend on palming.

IN MANY OF the coin tricks described in this manual, it is essential that a coin be palmed. This sleight is used to either produce, vanish, or secretly exchange or substitute a coin. Coins commonly used in this fashion range in denomination from a penny to a fifty-cent piece. The magical student should continue to practice these moves with a view to perfection. Most coin effects are entirely dependent upon this lone factor in sleight of hand.

Hold the coin on the tips of the second and third fingers in a balanced, horizontal position. Close the two fingers into the palm of your hand and push the coin into the cavity of your palm. Instantly exert pressure against the rim of the coin with the fleshy portion of your skin holding it into place. In a short time you will be able to determine just how to hold it for maximum security. Practice this standard palm so that you are able to deal cards and do a variety of things, using your fingers, and hands, with the coin (or coins) in a palmed position. Remember always to keep your hand relaxed and in a natural position. Never look at your fingers or hands when palming a coin, card, or any other small object. An audience generally follows your eyes and if you look at your hands, they, too, will look at them and detect what you are doing.

Misdirection is another important factor in sleight of hand. Always look away and in the direction of some apparatus other than that which you are using. In this fashion the audience will be guided by you automatically, and keep their eyes away from moves which are secretly essential to the performance of the trick. ★

thought reading

Anne Buccheri writes a message Dunninger will "thought read." Trick is not to be confused with telepathic powers.

Secret of this trick is in the top envelope; carbon paper transfers written message to paper when it's written upon.

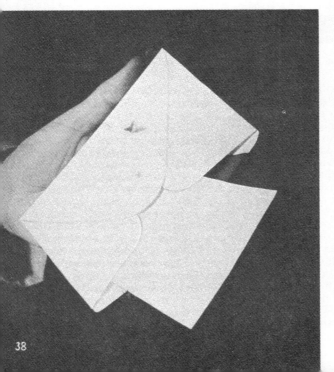

EXPERIMENTS IN thought reading are always desirable. This one is extremely simple.

Provide yourself with a package of envelopes, medium size. The package should have a paper band around it, as all envelopes have as they come untouched from the box. The top envelope of the bunch must be prepared as follows: place in the envelope a piece of carbon paper the size of the envelope; over this place a piece of plain white paper, the size of the envelope. Now, if you lay a piece of paper on the envelope and write upon it an impression will appear on the paper in the envelope.

To Perform: Advance to the company with this bunch of envelopes in your hand, also a pencil and slip of paper on top of the envelopes. Hand the prepared envelope, paper and pencil to some one in the audience with the request to write a message to some dead friend. As soon as they have finished writing you must in an off-hand manner take back the envelope and at same time request the party to fold up the paper. While he is doing this you must make the bottom change with the envelope. That is, you must quickly put the "carbon" envelope under the bunch of envelopes which you hold in your left hand, and with the same movement carry off with your right hand the top envelope—leaving the "carbon" envelope under bunch.

Hand the envelope to the party with the request to place the message in it, seal it and place in his pocket. If the change is neatly made the party will suppose she is sealing up the envelope you handed her first. In reality you have this envelope on bottom of the others, and in it a copy of the message. You retire with the envelopes and read the message and reveal it in any way you choose. ★

enchanted
handkerchief

THREE OR FOUR kerchiefs are displayed—various colored handkerchiefs add to the effect. The magician nonchalantly tosses the lot into the air and catches them as they descend. They are then found to have been mysteriously knotted together.

The helpful culprit is a small rubber band which is secretly held about the fingers as illustrated. The ends of the silks are held together in the same hand, covering the band. In the act of throwing them into the air, slip the rubber band over the bundle. At a short distance the illusion is perfect. ★

Performer can use any number of silks for this trick.

With a wave of the hand, the silks are tossed in air.

And when they land, they fall knotted together!

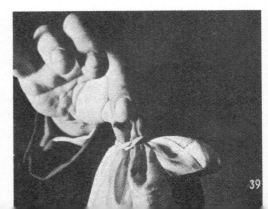

Secret of the trick is rubber band held as shown.

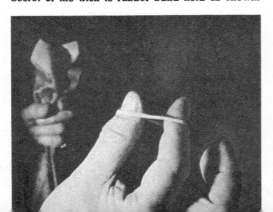

When silks are tossed, the band is flipped on ends.

patriotic billiard balls

Blindfolded, performer can determine ball's color.

Right, secret is a metal ball gauge beneath the coat.

Below, props needed: three colored balls, gauge.

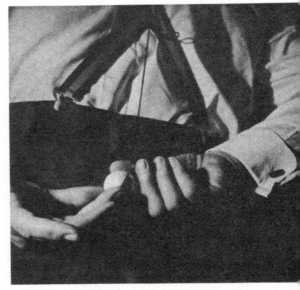

HERE IS A fine and somewhat different effect. Three billiard balls, approximately two inches in diameter, are passed for inspection. They are perfectly round and seem to differ only in respect to color. The magician is securely blindfolded before any one of the three colored balls is placed into his palm, held behind his back. Within a moment the magician calls the color of the ball he is holding. The trick is repeated as often as may be desired and during any stage of the experiment the spheres may be examined.

Secret: The balls vary slightly in size. This difference cannot be detected by the naked eye. The red ball is smallest, the white slightly larger and the blue the largest. Concealed beneath the magician's coat is a round steel ring attached to a piece of elastic. When the magician receives a ball from a spectator, he tests it with a ring. If the ball passes through the ring it is red, if it fits snugly it is white. The blue ball does not pass through at all. When the steel ring is released it flies up beneath the coat by means of an elastic cord. By applying several coats of enamel, the diameter of three balls of the same size can be varied sufficiently. ★

which hand?

Trick is for performer to leave the room, then re-enter and signify which hand has been elevated.

THIS impromptu experiment can be repeated many times with no danger of the method of operation being discovered.

The magician asks a spectator to take two coins and hold them in his hands. The spectator is seated and his hands rest on his knees. The magician then leaves the room. The spectator is asked to hold one of the coins up in front of his eyes for a count of twenty, while the magician is out of the room. When he returns he will tell the spectator which coin was observed.

The explanation is simple. While holding the coins on the knees the blood rushes to the hands and colors them slightly. In the hand that holds the coin in front of the eyes the blood recedes and leaves it lighter than the other. Try it. ★

Participant grasps coins on lap till magician leaves.

Secret: hand which is held up appears paler later.

The proper patter will aid this trick, and it's given in text. Secret is a thin thread, here highlighted by a side light. Ordinarily it is almost invisible.

is it hypnotism?

THE PERFORMER tells a story about the mysterious land of Tibet and the wonderful mystifying effect he learned from the lamas of that far-off land. A water glass is before him. As the story unfolds the magician performs the trick.

"Once upon a time," states the performer, "deep in the forbidding stone monasteries of Tibet, there lived a group of men who had forsaken the world. These men were students of the occult and had delved deeply into the many hidden mysteries of metaphysics.

"Hypnotism and mesmerism were practiced, so the story goes, and many are the miracles these men of the hills brought to light. One of the monks used to sit for hours at a time looking into a tumbler or glass like this. (Shows an ordinary glass tumbler.) He used this glass much as the crystal gazer or seer of today does—to seek hidden mysteries of the past, the present and the future. In the glass, partly filled with water drawn from a secret well, he looked for future happenings.

"One day, after unfolding to one of his colleagues a series of past events, the other monk told him of a number of startling experiments he had made while investigating and studying suspended animation. He also told a fantastic tale of how he

had levitated a large stone in front of the door of one of the cells a monk occupied. The other monk asked him if he couldn't see a demonstration of levitation.

"Agreeing, the monk took the glass and placed it on a table. He passed his hand over the glass. Slowly he raised his hand and the glass was seen to rise under some mysterious power. The higher the monk raised the hand the higher rose the glass. Awed, the other monk reached for the glass. But this broke the spell."

As the magician tells the last part of the story, the glass before him seemingly rises mysteriously in his hands before his amazed spectators. He hands out the glass for the spectators to examine, then shows his hands empty.

The mysterious power over the glass is easily explained. The glass is placed on the table. A number of passes are made over it. As the passes continue the hand is lowered above the glass and slipped through a piece of thread which extends around the glass. Slowly the glass is seen by the spectators to levitate below the hand. The other hand is then brought forward and grasps the glass, freeing it of the thread. The thread drops unseen to the floor and the glass is handed for inspection to the spectators. ★

latest
coin vanish

MAGICIANS ALWAYS seek a startling coin vanish. This one fills the bill. Carry a thread attached to a metal disc the size of a half-dollar up the left sleeve, across the back under the coat (fasten here with a safety pin) down the right sleeve and fasten it around right wrist. Smear wax on one side of the disc and hold disc in palm of left hand. When coin is laid on table, place hand over it. The coin will adhere to the disc and by a quick movement of spread of arms it will be drawn up the sleeve. The thread should be just long enough to allow the disc to be out of sight when the arms are apart. ★

Coin vanish is rigged with long thread attached to disc upon which is smeared a bit of adhesive wax.

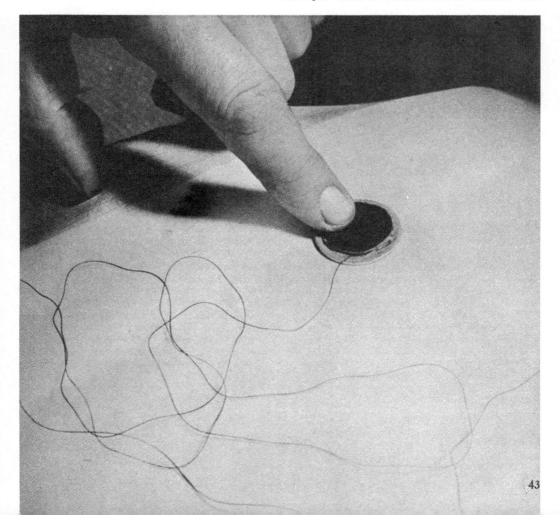

When deck of cards is thrown at ceiling, a predetermined card is found to adhere, while rest of deck falls to the floor. Secret is below—paste is smeared on the top card.

up-in-the-air card trick

AFTER HAVING a member of your audience select a card, you tell him to put it back in the deck. Now with all your skill, work the chosen card to the top of the deck. While you are having the card selected, you put your right hand into your right-hand pocket. This is necessary because in this pocket you have a little tin can which is one-third filled with ordinary ten-cent store paste. Deftly, you rub some of this paste on your second finger, and take your hand out of your pocket. When you receive the deck and have worked the se-

lected card to the top, you smear this bit of paste on the top card as you pretend to dovetail-shuffle the deck. Squaring the deck and holding it in your right hand, you throw the deck, giving it a slight twist, to the ceiling. And up she does go and there on the ceiling is the card chosen by the spectator. And there it will stay until you take it down. If there is a broom about, get it and retrieve the card yourself. This will give you an opportunity to wipe off the speck of paper paste. The tin box can be an aspirin tin. ★

THIS CLEVER COIN trick requires a little practice. It should not be presented until it is fully mastered. The performer puts a quarter in a handkerchief and holds it over a goblet. The quarter is dropped and apparently is heard to fall into the glass. Performer now draws the handkerchief around the edge of the glass and fastens it in place with a rubber band. Putting the glass on the table, performer waves his hand over it, and commands the coin to vanish. It does. *Secret:* Instead of dropping the coin into the glass, drop it so it strikes the base. As it falls, catch it and as you place the glass on the table with your right hand, secretly put the coin in your pocket with your left. ★

money flies

1: Props used for this trick are goblet, coin and silk.

2: With silk held over glass, coin is heard to fall.

3: Yet it's not in glass! It's really bounced off base.

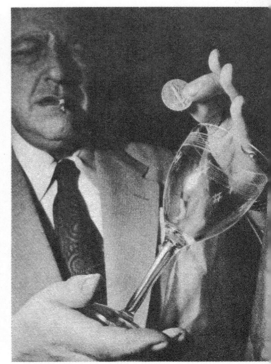

novel card rising effect

Cards selected by audience rise from the deck!

Below, the secret is in a rubber built-in wheel.

Below right, unseen by audience, card is raised.

IT SEEMS THAT for the past twenty-odd years, no one individual effect in magic has been accepted with as much emphasis of choice as the ever-popular rising-card trick. In this trick, cards previously chosen and shuffled back into the original deck mysteriously rise, in called-for rotation, from the deck without visible method.

I believe that my unique and practical method for bringing about the described illusion will be accepted by my many amateur and professional readers who, I trust, will appreciate the simplicity of this apparatus, together with its superiority over most complicated mechanical contrivances which have been offered to the wide-ranging field of mystics.

A number of cards, which have been glued together, act as a backing through which a small gear wheel has been affixed. This inexpensive arrangement can be constructed within a few moments by anyone with slight mechanical experience. Any number of cards, placed between this layer and the loose cards can be easily caused to rise by simply operating the gear with the index finger. Placing the cards in a case will help the handling considerably, as well as heighten the effect of presentation.

Duplicates to three or four cards which have been secretly arranged in front of the wheel are needed. These suits are, of course, forced on the unsuspecting spectators by any method the performer chooses. See page 30 for methods of card-forcing. ★

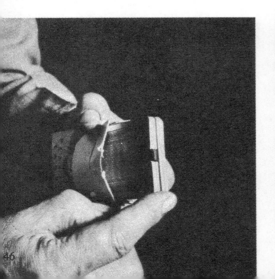

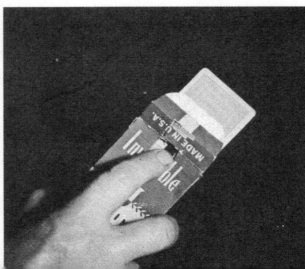

matchless fingers

Match box thrown in air ignites match on its fall!

T HIS SPECTACULAR effect consists of a new and mystifying way to light a cigarette. Picking up a box of matches, the magician extracts one, so it seems, and tosses the box into the air. As it descends the match is brought against the box and ignites.

Here is the way it's done. A solid block of wood is camouflaged with a label on top and "strike" paper on the bottom and sides —it really looks, from a few feet away, like just another of the strike-on-the-box variety of much used safety matches.

Seldom is it noticed that when the make-believe box is picked up from the table the match is also picked up and not extracted from the box. The magician tosses the box into the air with the left hand, the right holding the match at fingertips. He reaches out and up toward the box as it descends in the air, striking the match against the sides, or bottom of the box, and another bit of magic is neatly and efficiently accomplished.

In performing tricks, it must be remembered that what seems perfectly simple to you as a performer is extremely mystifying to the spectator, who doesn't know the trick's secret. Knowing the secret of a trick dilutes its entertainment value to the audience, so never reveal a trick's secret of you can help it. ★

Secret of trick is in the match box—it's really a block of wood covered with "strike" material on sides.

down for the count

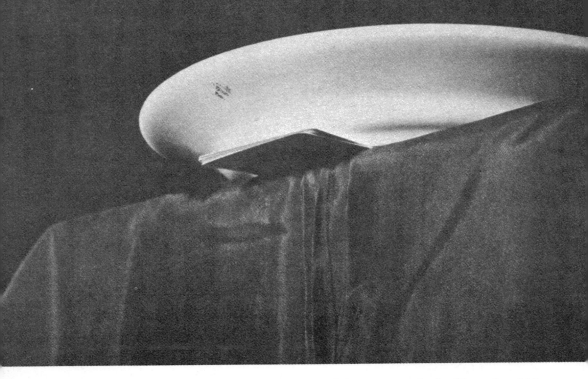

Three cards are secretly placed beneath a plate on the edge of a table in preparation for this numbers trick.

IN THIS EXPERIMENT you prove to the spectators that they are unable to count correctly. It has a humorous flourish.

Have three cards of any suit hidden under the rim of a small plate which rests on the edge of a table. Ask your assistant to drop 15 cards from a height of about a foot (so that all may see it's legitimate) onto the plate. Take up the plate, and with it the three hidden cards, covering their length with your fingers.

When your assistant has finished counting the cards onto the plate, bring the other hand up, fingers underneath thumb and, tilting the plate, allow the cards on the plate to fall into the waiting hand. At the same time allow the three cards at the back to slide down behind the 15. The first and little fingers of the hand gripping the plate, if held just beyond the sides of the three cards, will guide them into the other hand, preventing their slipping sideways.

The 15 cards should be dropped on the plate so they will spread out and afford ample cover for the three dropped from the back of the plate. ★

Cards beneath are secretly added to others for trick.

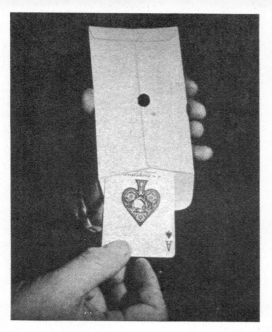

Card, envelope are shown to have matching holes.

After inserting card, draw ribbon through.

houdini ace

FOR THIS EXCEEDINGLY clever trick, you require an ordinary playing card with a hole in the center, a pay envelope, and a piece of ribbon about a yard long.

The card is placed inside the envelope and sealed. The ribbon is passed through the hole in the envelope and naturally passes through the hole in the center of the card. Yet when the end of the envelope is torn off, the card is mysteriously removed free and clear, leaving the ribbon.

The secret: When the card is pushed into the envelope it is shoved right through the bottom, which has previously and secretly been slit with a razor blade. The card projects through the envelope, slightly over half its length, but this deception is covered by the left hand which holds the bottom of the envelope. The ribbon is pushed through the envelope by the right hand, after which the right thumb pushes the card back into the envelope, which is then sealed.

In reality, the ribbon actually goes around the card and not through it, so that when the envelope is torn open the card can be easily removed. The envelope is left dangling upon the ribbon which runs through it. Tearing the envelope destroys evidence of preparation. ★

Card is withdrawn from envelope, ribbon remains!

Secret is in prepared envelope, slit at the bottom.

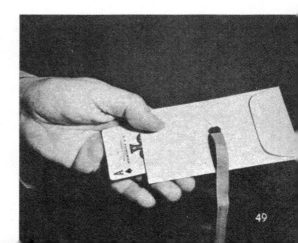

49

ghost frame

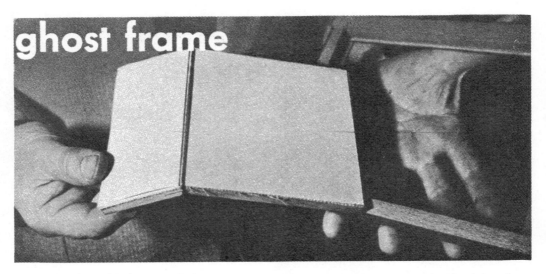

Hinged flap which fits into glass frame is shown to be completely blank before it is fitted into frame.

After frame is fastened, then lifted, writing appears! Secret is below—a hidden flap which falls into position.

THIS PARTICULAR offering was used by Houdini for a number of years and also holds the distinction of having mystified some of the cleverest and best-posted magicians in the country.

The prop is a large wooden frame in which is fixed a sheet of glass. A flap which opens is hinged to the frame. The flap being shown, and the glass being exhibited, the affair is closed and placed face down upon a table. After a few mystic passes, the frame is again exhibited—but now it contains a written message!

The explanation is this: In the act of closing the frame, a secret flap is permitted to fall, exposing the secretly written contents. With a little practice the magician can manipulate the apparatus with such dexterity that the action of causing the second flap to fall is unobserved. ★

20th century mind reading

Cards in a glass are mysteriously read by performer, although they are shuffled and faced away from him!

IN THIS EXPERIMENT, an unprepared deck of cards that can bear the closest of inspection is freely shuffled and placed in a glass tumbler, which is held at arm's length by the magician. In spite of the fact that the cards face the audience with their back to the performer, he mysteriously calls the exact rotation of the entire deck, reading the cards in front first, and removing one at a time as he reads them. Any deck will serve the purpose.

Like most good effects the trick is extremely simple, the magician having merely provided himself with a small mirror disk attached to a flesh colored band or ring. A small dental mirror will serve the purpose admirably. One merely need look at the index of the card and name it. ★

The secret is simple: a small dental mirror is palmed in a position where index of cards can be easily seen.

a good turn

This trick requires card-handling practice; first a card is forced upon a spectator, then put back in deck.

THIS IS A NOVEL method of producing a chosen card, completely different from the orthodox methods. The pack is dropped face down on the floor at a distance of three or four feet, and the chosen card appears face-up upon it.

Secret: We will assume that a card has been forced (see page 30) upon a spectator, and returned to the pack. Casually looking through the cards in the act of showing that they are all different, the magician secretly spots the card. He false-cuts the deck so as to permit the selected card to remain on top of the pack.

The card is pushed a little to one side, so that it overlaps; and the pressure of the air in falling will cause it to make a semi-revolution and appear face up on the pack, after the deck has been dropped to the floor. ★

"Spotted" force-card is brought to top of deck, then deck is false cut—top card is nudged to one side.

When deck is dropped, air pressure will flip the top card around; deck falls face down, chosen card up!

Three colored paper bands are looped onto a string.

A silk is thrown over string and choice is made.

chameleon bands

THIS PARTICULAR effect is really very simple, but because of this is more mystifying to the spectators. The magician displays three endless loops of differently colored paper on a string. Two spectators are requested to hold the opposite ends of the string. A large bandana is shown and the hands are covered with it. One of the spectators suggests a color; the performer mystically reaches beneath the handkerchief and removes the chosen colored band from the string, yet the band itself remains intact. *Secret:* The handkerchief has pockets sewn into its corners. The magician tears the selected colored band from the string, places it in the empty pocket. A corresponding intact paper band of the desired color is removed and shown. ★

Performer removes any band requested—intact!

Secret is in handkerchief—it has numerous pockets.

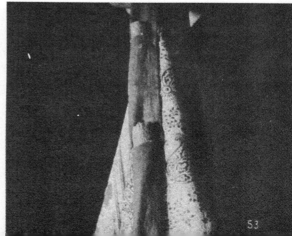

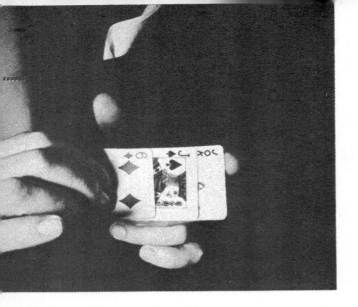

cards

At left are three photos which show Dunninger in the act of performing the trick: three cards are displayed, then squared as in the second photo. When the three cards are fanned out, the joker has turned into an ace of spades!

THIS CARD TRICK has actually fooled many well-posted magicians. Being of so simple a nature to construct, the writer feels that many students of the art will add it to their repertoire, which is well worth the little time spent to make the necessary preparation.

The effect consists of displaying three cards with the request that your audience memorize their suits. Cards are then squared and without any suspicious move placed face down upon the table. The performer requests that the spectators repeat the values of the cards memorized. Two of the cards still retain their suits, but the third is found to have changed. This card can bear inspection.

Preparation: Five cards are used. The jack and the four are hinged by means of a narrow strip of paper. The jack is then brought over and glued down upon a strip. This affair now forms a "pocket" card which can be freely shown from either

illusional

At right are three photos which show how the trick is accomplished. The jack is actually a "pocket" card, made from two cards, in which the joker, a half-card, is sandwiched. Behind this is hidden the ace, seen below.

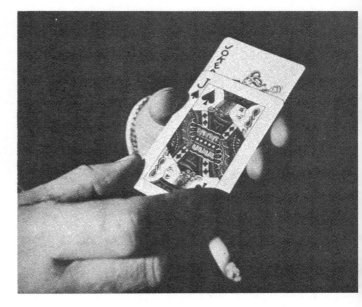

side and displayed as one. The pocket card contains a portion of the joker. This half card is a trifle narrower so as to slide easily in and out of the pocket card. The six and the ace are regulation cards.

Presentation: Before presenting this trick, the trick cards are arranged face-up in the following order: the six, the jack "pocket" card (with the joker jutting out of the pocket card and an ace behind this). When shown, however, the ace is kept concealed behind the pocket card. The spectators are asked to memorize the three cards they see, which are the six, jack, and joker. When cards are brought together and placed face down on the table, the joker is, of course, automatically forced into the "pocket" made for it and disappears from sight. When the cards are picked up again and fanned out, the ace is now the third card in the position formerly occupied by the joker. The ace can be passed for inspection. ★

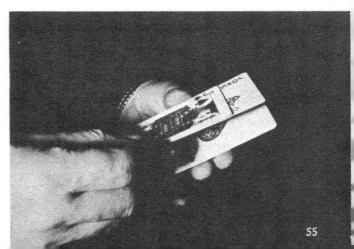

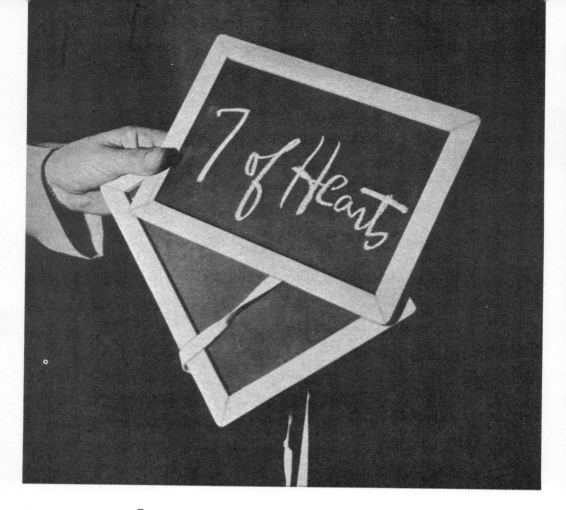

spirit slates

The name of a previously forced card (see page 30) or any message can be mysteriously inscribed.

HERE is a mystifying experiment in mystic spiritual writing which will astound your audience. Two thin slates are brought forth and offered for examination by the audience. The performer then places in between the two plates a small piece of chalk and hands the two slates to someone in the audience to tie with a string or seal all around with sealing wax. After a few minutes or so the slates are taken apart and presto!—there is found a message from the "spirit world" written with the chalk placed in there by the Medium.

Here's the way it's done: the chalk is special. It is made of chalk dust mixed with iron filings and a little glue. A strong (need not be large) magnet is used to make the chalk move and write the message. The Medium locates the chalk by tipping the slates to one corner and placing the magnet under it.

This works better in the dark for the simple reason that the people will not notice the magnet and its use. Should the magician decide to present the effect in full daylight, the slate can be held beneath the table during the action of creating the mystic writing. In this event, a tiny magnet fixed to a flesh-colored band or a ring is substituted for the larger magnet. ★

The slates are shown to be unmarked before the trick begins. Chalk is then placed between the slate boards. This trick is best performed in a dark room.

With no false movements, the slates are tied and sealed; the seals can be marked by any skeptical observers who can inspect again before the climax.

With a strong magnet, the performer writes the message. Chalk is located by tilting the slates, sliding chalk to the corner; this is done under cover.

Secret to the trick is the chalk: it's specially made of a mixture of chalk dust, iron filings and glue. A smaller magnet, palmed, can be used in daylight.

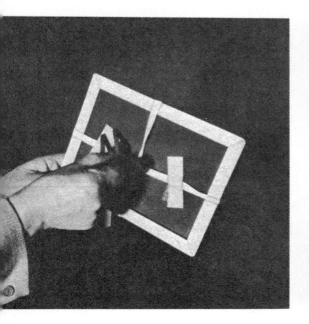

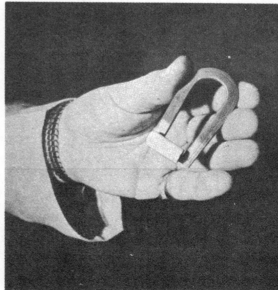

four ace miracle

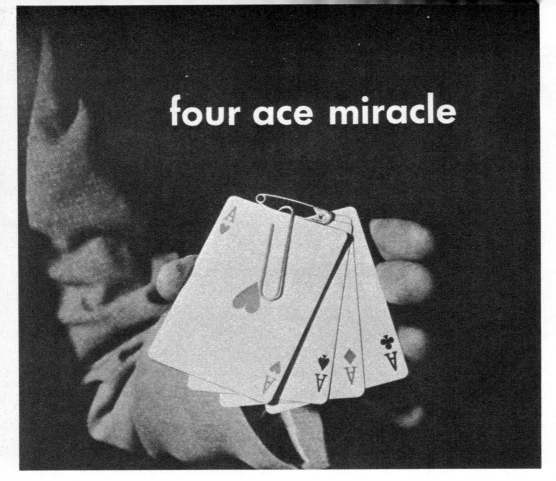

Aces are separated and prepared as shown.

Deck behind back, aces are "called," then drawn.

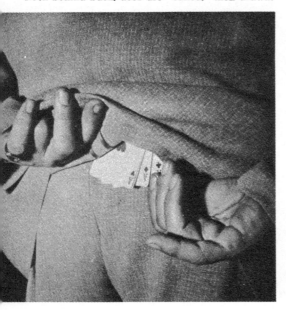

THIS IS QUITE an effective and easily performed card trick. A spectator thoroughly shuffles a deck. The performer takes the deck and holds it behind his back. He now announces the ace of spades, removes one card from behind his back and it is the correct suit as called. In rapid succession he produces the other three aces, announcing their names accurately before producing them from behind his back. At the conclusion of the trick the entire pack may be examined.

Secret: The four aces have been previously removed. Memorize their order and then attach them to an ordinary paper clip. The clip is then attached to a safety pin which is fastened to the lining in back of your coat, about one inch above the edge of the coat, so the cards can't be seen. Hold the deck behind your back with one hand and use the other to remove the aces.

When the deck is originally shuffled no one will suspect that the aces are missing as the spectators are not familiar with what you intend to do. Later, examination of the pack is invited. ★

card in hat mystery

Below, magician's view of hat as trick is prepared.   A tap of the hat brings the called card bouncing out.

A TRULY UNIQUE and mystifying effect can be done with a deck of cards and a soft fedora hat. The surprising finish will amaze spectators. From a pack of cards the performer chooses one, shows it and then returns it to the pack. He looks through it again for the chosen card, but seemingly fails to find the card in the pack; he drops the pack into a soft hat, holds the hat above his head, and snaps his finger against the bottom of the crown. The chosen card instantly flies from the hat.

The explanation for this interesting feat is really very simple. The crown of a soft hat has two compartments. In looking for the chosen card, the performer actually finds it, then drops the pack in one section of the hat and the chosen card in the other section. When he snaps his finger against the section that contains the single card, that card will fly in the air. I would suggest that an effective and practical method of locating the chosen card would be to employ method as explained on page 106. ★

A finger in a box is exhibited and said to be the digit of a long-dead king—yet the finger lives!

pharaoh's finger

READERS should have no hesitation in adding this remarkable effect to their box of tricks. The magician explains that years ago, while in Egypt, a caravan trailing its way through the sands of the deserts rested for a few brief moments within the shadows of the pyramids. The magician, who had been traveling through the Holy Land in search of things mystic, met the chief of this tribe and befriended him. Months later, the chief found himself in a position which threatened his life, and the magician saved him. In payment, the chief presented him with a finger which was said to have been at one time affixed to the hand of one of the Pharaohs, dead these thousands of years. The finger, he explains, although mummified, possesses a strikingly lifelike appearance. All this time the magician has held in his hands a small Oriental figured box. The spectators are at this time requested to gather about the performer. Slowly, and with much ceremony, he now lifts the lid of the box. There, resting upon a small pillow of white cotton, the audience sees a severed finger so natural, so lifelike, that it is startling and uncanny. They are permitted to feel this finger, and to their absolute amazement find it to possess natural human warmth in accordance with the magician's description. Carefully the box is closed, and carried to a chest, where it is locked away.

The explanation: The finger is none other than that of the performer, who sticks it through a hole in the bottom of the treasure chest. Holding it in his outstretched hand, this deception is quite unnoticed. The bedding of cotton helps considerably to perfect the illusion, and likewise conceals the edges of the finger hole. Those who do not choose to construct a box with ancient markings will find a jeweler's plush box easily available, and as effective. ★

The secret is in the box—a concealed hole permits the performer to use his own finger for the trick.

Performer of this trick sets a lump of sugar burning.

Secret of burning sugar: dip sugar lump in ashes.

burning sugar

DUNNINGER has used this after-dinner trick for a number of years and has never found anyone who has discovered its secret without being in the know. The performer requests the members of his group to attempt to light a lump of sugar using an ordinary match. No matter how hard they will try, as you will find upon experimentation, the sugar will sizzle and blacken, yet will not flame. The ma- gician uses a lump from the same bowl, yet finds little or no difficulty in causing it to burn freely. All you need know to perform this trick is to remember to dip the end of the sugar you use into a nearby ash tray, causing a small quantity of ashes to cling to the sugar. That's the end you burn and the only piece in the lot that will flame away briskly. When dipping the sugar lump, do it casually and unseen. ★

A spectator, uninformed, will try the same stunt time after time with no success. Ashes aid combustion.

The cards are riffled under the eyes of a spectator; it is seen that every card in the deck is a red one!

An instant later the cards are riffled once again; this time every card flipped appears to be black!

color card mystery

HERE IS AN excellent card mystery which requires a pack of fifty-two cards and the joker, prepared beforehand.

The performer displays a pack of cards with the joker on the face. He states that the cards are all red—that is, with the exception of the joker. To prove this, he riffles the end of the pack, rather slowly, and shows that all the cards are red.

Then he breathes upon the pack, and says that the red cards have all become black. He riffles the cards and shows that they are all black! He finally commands the pack to become both red and black, which it does—for when the cards are riffled, some are red and others are black. The entire pack may be passed for examination.

The secret: First separate the red and black cards of the pack. Lay the joker *aside.* Then shuffle the reds and the blacks together, by riffling the ends, very slowly, so that cards are practically alternating red and black. Push the two halves of the pack together, but stop before they are quite flush. Then place the joker on the face of the pack, and have the cards in readiness.

When you pick up the pack, you will find that if you hold the cards firmly in your left hand, and riffle one end with your right hand, only one color will show. That is because the cards of that color protrude, and the other cards fall behind them. Thus you show the pack to be either all red or all black, as the case may be. When you turn the pack around and riffle the opposite end, the other color will appear. To finish the trick, it is necessary to slide the two sections of the pack together until they are flush; then both colors generally-mixed will show when the pack is riffled. ★

Secret: a stacked deck with the joker in front; reds and blacks are alternated and separated as shown.

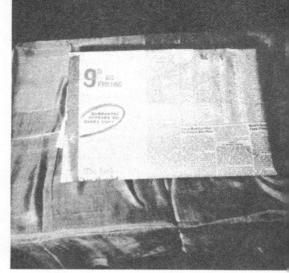

Slate is casually wrapped in paper; picture shows prepared paper (left) which is concealed from audience.

spirit writing

A FINE TRICK with a surprising effect is this one which concerns spirit-slate writing. The magician wraps an unprepared slate in a previously prepared piece of paper. A message is written on the piece of paper with the edge of a hard piece of soap; write the message on the area which will come in contact with the slate, and do it out of sight of your audience, of course. The message in soap is written in reverse—as it would appear in a mirror if written in ordinary fashion, for example.

After the reverse writing is made on the slate, the soap letters are saturated with chalk dust. Thus, when the slate is wrapped in the paper, and the paper is rubbed several times with the hand (apparently to smooth it), the writing is transferred to the slate. You can create "spirit messages" or the name of a selected card. ★

When the slate is unwrapped, the name of a previously selected card has mysteriously been written upon its surface! Secret: message is written on paper in reverse with soap, chalk dust.

living
or
dead

HERE IS A spectacular mental effect that mystifies all spectators, a clever impromptu effect requiring no special apparatus which makes it all the more convincing to those watching.

The magician supplies his spectators with eight or nine small visiting cards. He requests all of them to write the name of living persons whom he does not know upon the cards, with the exception of one spectator who is requested to write the name of a dead person on the card. The cards are dropped into a hat, and the magician on picking them out announces the name of the dead person. The penciled writings give him the clue. The magician gives the spectator writing the name of the dead person a hard lead pencil; all the others get soft pencils. ★

handkerchief
penetration

Water is poured into glass to prove all is well; actually, the thumb covers a hole in bottom side.

THIS IS A startling experiment, well worthy of the slight amount of preparation it requires. A handkerchief, a small glass tumbler, and an ornamental open-ended cardboard cylinder cover are shown. From a transparent glass pitcher the tumbler is filled to the brim with water. The water is then poured back into the pitcher, handkerchief is placed in the glass and the tube placed over the tumbler. Immediately the handkerchief is pulled out at the bottom, having apparently penetrated the glass tumbler. The glass is at once filled with water again, proving beyond doubt that it is an ordinary tumbler.

One in audience has put name of dead man in hat.

It is detected; magician gave writer special pencil.

Secret: The tumbler is prepared by having a piece about the size of a quarter cut out of one side, at the bottom. On the table have the pitcher filled with water, the tube cover, the glass, and the handkerchief. Take the glass in your left hand, covering the hole cut in the side of the glass at the bottom with your thumb.

From the pitcher pour water into the glass, then back into the pitcher again, convincing the spectators that the glass is unprepared. Now take the handkerchief and push it inside the glass, taking care that a little part of the handkerchief protrudes at the round opening at the bottom, which will facilitate pulling it out. Put the cylinder over the glass so that the end of the handkerchief shows at the top. Now grasp the protruding handkerchief from the other side of the cylinder and pull until it is entirely out. Throw it on the table, taking off the tube cover at the same time. Put your thumb over the opening in the glass, again fill it with water, and empty it back into pitcher, proving the glass to be without preparation. ★

Tube is placed over glass, kerchief pulled through.

Glass cutter can be used to make the prop glass.

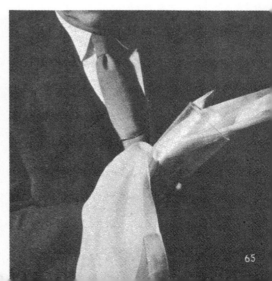

65

The performer is blindfolded before selecting a cigarette previously called by a spectator.

weird touch

CIGARETTE TRICKS are ever popular, particularly with an after dinner crowd. This one will prove an extremely effective impromptu offering.

Take five or six cigarettes of different manufacture and state that the audience may select a brand name, and that you, while blindfolded with a handkerchief, will pick that selected cigarette out of a hat. *The secret:* After the cigarette brand name is verbally selected, have someone hand you the different cigarettes. Note the one with the selected name. Just as you drop this cigarette into the hat, crimp it a little in the center. To find it, all you have to do is to feel which cigarettes are hard, round, and normal, and which one has the slight crimp. ★

Without hesitation, the brand called is selected! Secret of the trick: a crimp is made beforehand.

elusive ace

THE FOLLOWING effect is an easily constructed, highly-mystifying trick. Three cards: the ace of spades and two court cards are shown resting on a black velvet stand built in easel fashion about 14 inches wide by 7 inches high. A thin strip of wood is nailed along the lower edge to form a ledge upon which the cards may rest. In presenting the effect the three cards mentioned are slowly shuffled. The audience is requested to follow the position of the ace. With their backs toward the audience the cards are arranged upon the stand, whereupon any member is requested to call the position of the ace. Regardless of the choice made, when the card called for is turned face upward it proves to be one of the court cards. Regardless of the number of tries the location of the elusive ace is never discovered by the spectators.

Explanation: Six cards are used—the three originally shown and three court cards of the same suit as two of the cards in the first group. The latter are backed with black velvet. These three cards (velvet side facing the audience) are arranged upon the stand, and at a short distance are invisible. The three unprepared cards are arranged upon the rack—each card directly upon the top of a velvet-covered card. Therefore, regardless of where the ace of spades may be when the choice is made, the magician has but to turn over the two cards as though they were one. Obviously the chosen card always proves to be a court card. ★

Above, felt-backs are unseen when in place.

Real cards are placed over felt-backs, then when spectator calls for card seen, phony is shown.

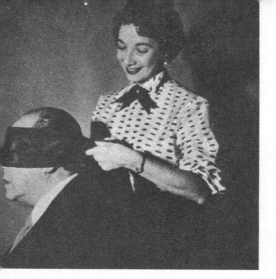

second sight

THIS IS RATHER a startling and exceptional effect, and perhaps one of the very few that has mystified some of the cleverest of present day magicians. Tricks of this kind are exceptionally rare. I hope my readers will not be misled as to its value by the simplicity of its secret.

A deck of cards is thoroughly shuffled, and placed in the crown of a borrowed hat. The magician requests the loan of another hat, which is placed upon the first, rim to rim, and the cards are thoroughly shaken up between the crowns of the two hats, by one of the spectators. This voluntary assistant is now requested to return the upper hat of the two to its owner, and cover the other hat containing the cards with a previously examined and unprepared handkerchief. The magician is blindfolded, then led to a table supporting the hat, cards and handkerchief.

He slowly draws a card from the hat and names it correctly. In this manner the magician mysteriously calls the names of 10 or 12 cards and produces them in accurate succession from out of the hat. The cards, hat and handkerchief are again passed for inspection but there are no clues to be found that would explain the mystery.

The secret, in this case, as in many other magical mysteries, is exceptionally simple. The magician has previously memorized and placed in rotation 10 or 12 cards, which are held together with a paper clip. This stack, after being placed together with the balance of the deck is shuffled by means of the old-fashioned hand-to-hand shuffle in order not to disturb the stack.

While blindfolded the performer reaches under the cover of the handkerchief, finds this stack among the rest and calls them in memorized rotation as they are produced. A slight bend in the clip will make it possible for him to distinguish the face from the backs of the cards. ★

After the performer is blindfolded, he is handed a handkerchief-covered hat in which a deck of cards has previously been thoroughly shaken by a skeptic; without a pause, he draws a dozen cards and names them correctly. Paper clip aids secret.

Dunninger's magic wand is made to assume positions that defy the law of gravity, yet it passes inspection.

stick magnet

Secret is not on wand but on clothes—see below.

IN THIS UNIQUE experiment the magician mysteriously makes his small wand assume various positions seemingly without outside aid. After passing the wooden wand for inspection, the magician causes it to adhere to the fingertips, to the palm or back of the hand.

A fine silk thread and a weight are responsible. The thread leads down through the magician's shirt front into the leg of his trousers where a small weight is affixed. The weight holds the thread under constant tension thus allowing the magician to cause the wand to assume the various mysterious positions.

Needless to say, at a very short distance the spectators cannot see the fine silk thread that operates the effect. As in all effects requiring the use of a silk thread, the black clothes of the magician as a background to the thread aid its invisibility.

As a point of interest to the beginning magician, it might be said that when preparing a program of tricks, the number of illusions which will employ thread or other openly concealed devices should be taken into consideration. If they are many, a black dinner jacket may be a good investment for you. ★

yogi coin vanish

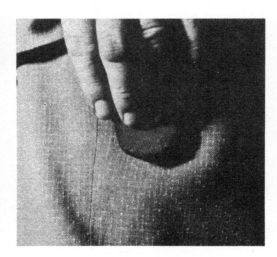

A secret receptacle which can be fastened to the clothing is the basis for the Yogi Coin Vanish trick. A number of coins can be made to disappear singly or all at once. It's best to have the box covered with material or paint the color of clothes worn so it'll blend in properly and remain unseen when trick is performed.

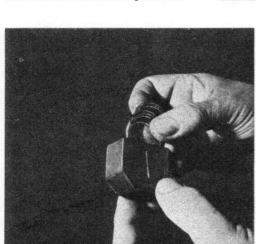

AN EXPERIMENT high in mystification, yet easy to perform, is this one. Five or six half-dollars are freely shown between the performer's fingers while sleeves are rolled to the elbows. They are stacked in the right hand and gently placed in the left. Both front and back of hands are freely shown a moment later and coins have mysteriously vanished.

A metal fake receptacle, lined and covered with cloth, is the apparatus responsible for bringing about this pretty effect. To the upper edge of this fake is permanently affixed a sharp pointed hook, as illustrated. This fake is secretly gotten in possession of and it is in this the coins are quietly nested, the fingers of the performer's hands forming an outer screen to conceal the action. The coins are apparently transferred from the right hand into the left, but in reality are retained, together with fake, in the right hand, and with a half turn to the right the hand holding coins is permitted to drop naturally to the artist's side, which action offers him an opportunity to get rid of the fake by catching the hooked end of same to his trousers leg. Both hands are gradually shown empty; the believability and neatnes of this action depends upon the ability of the performer and the practice devoted to perfecting this move. When of similar material to the performer's clothing this fake is quite unnoticeable, and with a little practice it can be attached to the trousers leg as to be covered by the performer's coat. ★

Three aces are shown, then shuffled into the deck.

Ace of diamonds shows up in pocket! See above.

traveling ace

HERE IS a good trick that if cleverly done will amaze your audience. The performer exhibits three aces—spades, clubs and diamonds, with the ace of diamonds between the other two. He inserts these aces face down in various portions of the pack. He then asks the spectators to choose either the red or the black aces. Suppose the red ace of diamonds is chosen. The pack is spread out, but the ace is not there! It proves to be in the performer's pocket.

The explanation is simple. The ace of diamonds is placed in the pocket before the trick begins. What appears to be the ace of diamonds is really the ace of hearts, which is held between the two black aces and in back of them so that only the point of the center heart is in view.

The cards, after being shown, are turned face down so that they may be inserted separately in the pack. If the red ace of diamonds is chosen, the performer makes it "pass" to his pocket. If the black aces are chosen, he says, "That leaves me the ace of diamonds. You will find your aces in the pack. Mine is here in my pocket!" Then he brings forth the ace of diamonds. ★

jumping cigar band

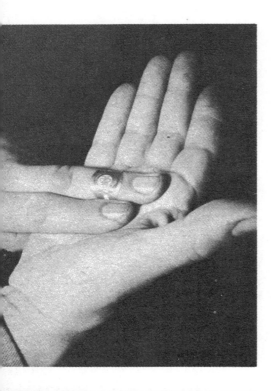

UNQUESTIONABLY, this is one of the cleverest pocket tricks yet invented. The magician places an ordinary cigar band upon the tip of the second finger of his right hand. He explains that he has the ability to magically cause the band to fly instantaneously from one finger tip to another.

He places his index finger and second finger (with the band) close together at the edge of the palm of his left hand. The other fingers are curled in. He brings the hand up and down with short sudden movements and at the same time secretly curls his index finger into the hand and brings up the third finger. It now appears that the band has actually jumped from one finger to another.

In reality he has just substituted the third finger for the first one. The audience cannot detect the move, owing to the speed of the up and down movement. Repeat the effect several times and you will find that the band actually seems to jump from finger to finger. This trick really proves that the hand is quicker than the eye. ★

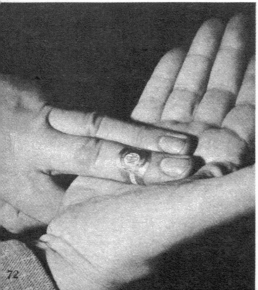

With quick hand movements, a cigar band on the second finger of the left hand can be made to apparently jump from one finger to another; note illustrations.

houdini match trick

ON MANY occasions, Harry Houdini discussed his famous Water Torture Cell illusion. My readers are undoubtedly familiar with the effect in which Houdini freed himself from a large water-filled tank after being securely fastened therein in an upside down position.

Houdini's favorite follow-up to this conversation was to claim and sometimes wager that he could light an ordinary match under water.

After all were assured that the feat was impossible, Houdini would simply fill a glass of water and then light a match under the glass, making good his claim.

Although this is not a magic trick in the true sense of the word, we believe it has earned a place among devotees of Houdini's favorite effects. ★

Houdini's sense of humor is evident in this trick; following a weighty discussion about his famous Water Cell illusion, he'd light a match underwater—simple?

enchanted saltshaker

HERE is an effective after-dinner trick which may be performed anywhere. No previous preparation is necessary. In effect, the magician is seen to place his finger tips upon the cap of a saltcellar, and then slowly raise it into the air.

Secret: The magician during the course of the meal finds an opportunity to secrete a toothpick beneath his finger ring.

First he calls attention to the saltcellar. Then, holding the toothpick firmly, he stretches his finger tips over the saltcellar and forces the point into one of the holes in the cap. The back of his hand is facing the audience to conceal the toothpick. After he has lifted the saltcellar, he can let the toothpick drop to the floor unnoticed. ★

Secretly, the performer places toothpick in shaker.

Hand shielding toothpick, performer lifts shaker.

To all outward appearances, shaker is enchanted.

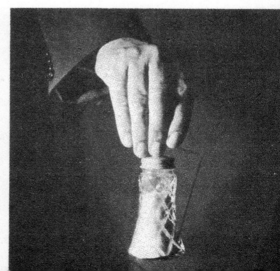

Participant is asked to concentrate on object placed on star center.

When magician returns, he is able to tell what object, now **hidden**, was. Secret is luminous paint applied to star

witchcraft

THIS entirely new trick can be presented as an impromptu mystery. The apparatus consists of a five-pointed star painted on a red card.

After relating some plausible tale describing the mysterious powers of the stars, the entertainer requests a spectator to place some object on the star and gaze at it while the magician leaves the room. The spectator is then to pick up the object and secrete it in his pocket. Upon his return, the magician picks up the star, and goes into a corner of the room. He requests concentration and then announces to the audience the article thought of by the spectator.

Secret: The star is painted with luminous paint and shows by shadow what the object was. Walking to a dark corner enables the performer to see the shadow more clearly. ★

the plate eater

The performer begins and ends with a whole plate, yet during trick a piece is bitten off and restored!

THE MAGICIAN CHATS about East Indian tribes who feast upon stones, metal and the like. He picks up a large white china plate, and without hesitation apparently bites off a large piece. The action produces a loud snap as though the plate were breaking. Then the magician seems to swallow the piece. Next, holding the plate in front of his stomach, he rubs the missing section with his fingers whereupon the plate is mysteriously restored to its original form.

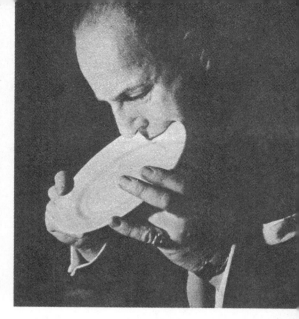

Sequence photos show how trick is accomplished; above left photo shows step to be taken secretly. Piece is placed over plate just prior to "bite." To "restore" plate, the metal piece is palmed away.

Secret: An irregular, bite-sized piece of metal is slid over the edge of the plate just before the magician puts the plate into his mouth. When the conjurer removes the plate from his mouth and holds it up against his dark suit, the illusion of the missing piece is perfect.

The snap is produced by clicking a coin or a ring against the back of the plate. The plate is made "whole" again by palming the metal piece.

Naturally, the metal piece should be a dead black if the magician commonly uses a black suit for his performance; a slight distance from the audience is desirable to guarantee success for the illusion. ★

a sweet trick

THIS ALWAYS FOOLS friends; it is very good as an after-dinner trick. Place a piece of sugar on end in a full cup of coffee. Now, before calling attention to what you are doing, place another piece of sugar on top of the concealed lump.

Point now to the fact that this piece of sugar is "floating" on top. Then, as your audience watches, command it to sink slowly from sight. Naturally, as the lower (unseen piece) melts, the floating lump must sink. Don't have the coffee too hot, or the sugar will dissolve too rapidly. ★

Unnoticed, the performer of this trick stacks two lumps of sugar in a cup of coffee in the shape of a "T" (left) so that the sugar lump appears to float. After calling it to the attention of the spectators, magician makes the lump "vanish" with a pass.

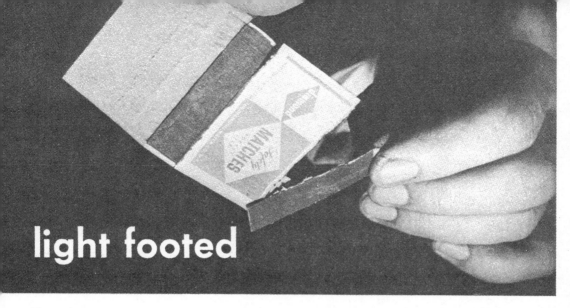

light footed

The performer prepares for this trick beforehand by first removing the strike portion from safety match box.

IT IS COMMONLY supposed that a safety match cannot be struck other than on its original box. The magician, however, upon meeting a friend who requests a light, or in front of an audience, amazes the spectators by striking this match upon the sole of his shoe and then challenges others to duplicate the feat. Try as they will, they will find it impossible to do.

The secret is exceedingly simple. The striking side of a match box was previously rubbed against the performer's shoe at the instep. Some of the substance is in this manner transferred from the box to the shoe. As the instep does not touch the ground in walking the application will not wear off for quite a time. Inasmuch as the magician knows that his friends have not previously prepared their shoes, he is free to challenge them without fear of the feat being duplicated. Try this one at your next party. ★

The strike material is rubbed into instep of shoe.

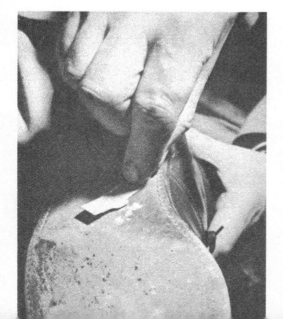

This allows magician to light safety match on shoe.

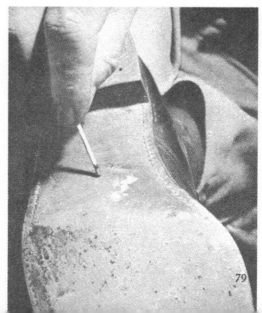

banknote mystery

The right index finger over bill indicates number 1.

Two fingers placed over bill (below) mean number 2.

Three fingers of right hand over bill mean number 3.

Four fingers of right hand are the sign for number 4.

Holding bill in center with right hand indicates 5.

Index finger of the left hand indicates number 6.

THIS EXPERIMENT in mind reading requires a bit of practice and a large amount of concentration, but the results are well worth the effort. I have found it puzzling to many men well-versed in the art of conjuring.

The mind-reader has an assistant who requests a bill from a spectator. The assistant explains that the mind-reader will call all the numbers upon the bill without speaking with the assistant before or during the performance.

To allay suspicions the mind-reader stands at a distance of 20 or 30 feet from his assistant. The assistant holds the bill between his fingers and at once the mind-reader mysteriously calls the exact serial numbers.

Secret: A signal finger system is employed. By straightening the bill repeatedly and changing the position of his fingers, the assistant informs the mind-reader of the proper figures in their correct sequence.

The illustrations clarify the method employed. While the assistant signals the digits, the mind-reader may use various dramatic gestures of concentration to hold audience attention upon himself. Properly performed, this mental stunt will thoroughly amaze and amuse spectators. ★

Two fingers of the left hand on the bill mean 7.

Three fingers of the left hand on bill mean 8.

Four fingers of the left hand holding bill is 9.

Zero is indicated by holding the bill from the top.

making money

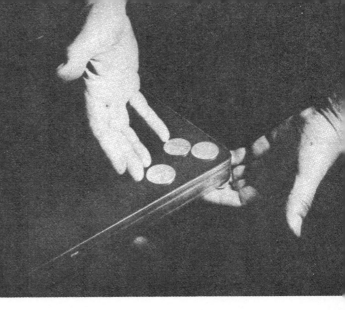

Three coins placed on edge of table can turn to four coins when this mystifier is properly performed.

THIS CHOICE after-dinner trick is extremely easy to perform. Place three coins on a table. Roll up your sleeves. Now cup your left hand on the side of the table. With your right hand, move the three coins into the left. Now ask a friend to blow on your hand; as he does, slowly open your hand. Show four coins instead of three!

Secret: An extra coin is attached with wax or a bit of gum under the table. The fingers of the performer's left hand reach under the table and pick up the hidden coin as the three other coins on top of the table are being moved toward the left hand. ★

Secret is obvious to everyone except the audience—a coin is fastened beneath the table. The hand must be fast for this trick; for proper cover right hand hides left.

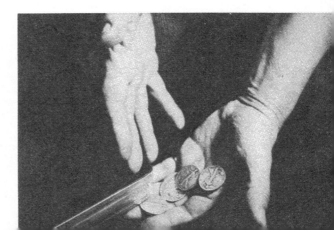

coin in
the orange

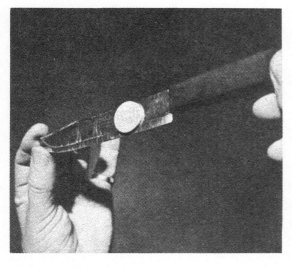

Here, Anne Buccheri, production editor for Fawcett Books, selects a solid, fool-proof looking orange.

FOR THIS beautiful effect, the requirements are a tray of oranges, a sharp table knife and a table. Request a spectator to freely select an orange. After the fruit has been proven to be intact, it is given to the spectator to hold. Now vanish a twenty-five-cent piece (by any method explained in this volume). Upon cutting the orange in two the actual quarter (marked) is discovered inside.

To prepare for this trick, a duplicate to the vanished coin is secretly pasted to the back of the knife with a daub of wax. The knife is laid on the table with the coin beneath. When cutting the orange the knife is held as illustrated and the coin secretly pushed down into the orange.

The original marked coin which has apparently vanished is now palmed and substituted for the duplicate from within the orange. The original is returned to the spectator from whom it had been borrowed. There is sufficient orange juice remaining upon the magician's fingers, which he rubs into the marked coin upon its return, so that a skeptical spectator might check the coin by smell. ★

But Dunninger produces a coin from the orange—using the method shown in the photos. The coin is actually attached to the knife, then concealed prior to slicing.

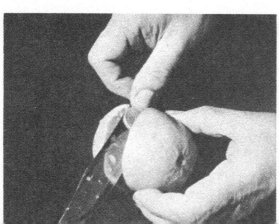

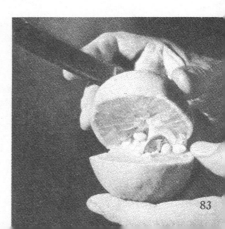

balancing coin trick

THE PRETTY EFFECT of mysteriously catching half dollars on the edge of a seemingly unprepared playing card has always impressed novelty-seeking magicians. This trick, however, has often been eliminated due to clumsy and inaccurate working mechanical cards. I have designed and have used to advantage for a number of years a simple and inexpensive card device for bringing about this effect successfully.

Secret: By referring to the photographs, one will clearly understand the construction of this unique piece of apparatus. Upon the

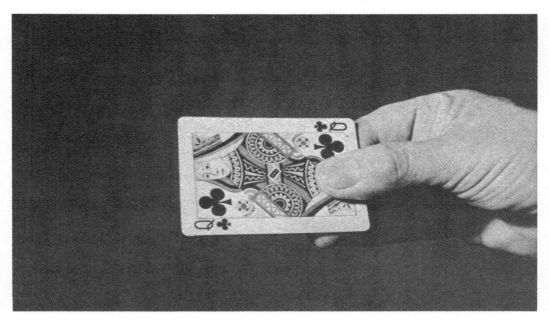

A seemingly unprepared card is shown on both sides. A coin is also shown, then with hocus-pocus . . .

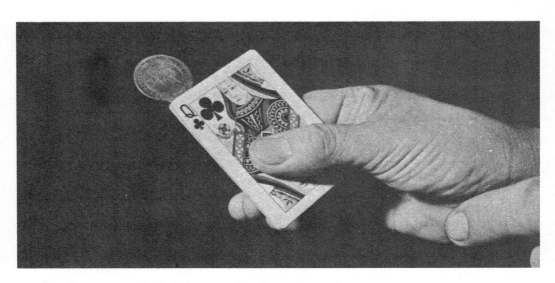

. . . the coin appears to be in balance on the edge of the card. Trick secret is in card (see photo, left).

back of an ordinary playing card are glued three cards cut as shown. To this is attached a lever or small metal arm to the free end of which a half dollar sized coin is permanently affixed. Another unprepared card is glued directly on top of this arrangement. This card may be displayed from either side, impressing one that it is quite unprepared, yet when it is firmly held between the fingers at a corner and given a sharp jerk the coin will appear at the upper edge of the card. When the coin is apparently removed it is, in reality, pushed back into its original hiding place, being substituted by one previously palmed in the other hand. This action may be repeated as often as desired, giving the effect of catching several coins in rotation. ★

spirited magic

1: Toy balloon filled with wine should be prepared beforehand.

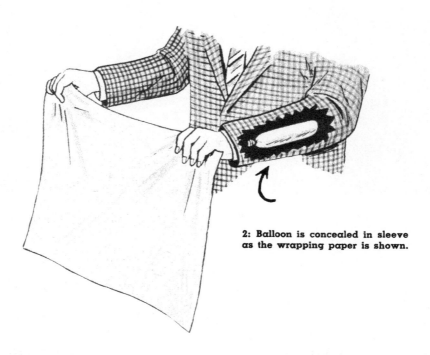

2: Balloon is concealed in sleeve as the wrapping paper is shown.

HERE'S AN ORIGINAL experiment that with a little practice can be executed with signal success. This type of effect is extremely suitable for those possessing a basement drinking bar.

However, whether you possess such a bar or not is truly immaterial as the experiment is an especially mysterious one under any conditions. A paper is rolled into the form of a tube. Both ends are twisted up and the tube is cut through the center with a pair of scissors. Wine flows out of the tube, filling two glasses and the paper is then crushed and thrown away.

In the sleeve of the performer's coat, a rubber toy balloon filled with wine is placed. This is secretly introduced into the paper roll while it is being formed. The balloon remains in the paper when it is thrown away. ★

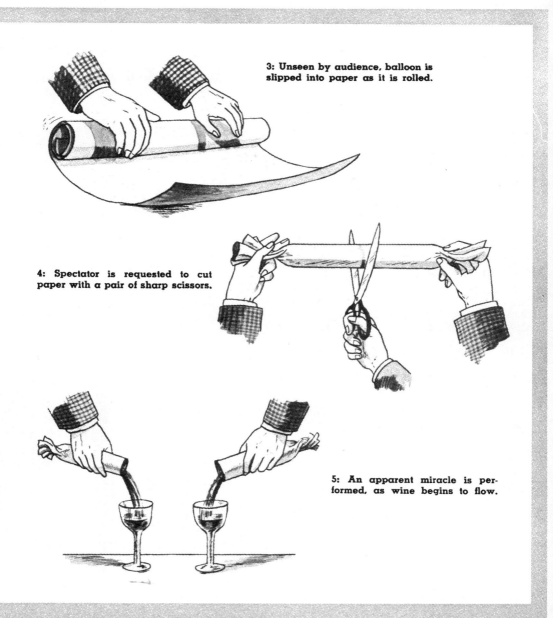

3: Unseen by audience, balloon is slipped into paper as it is rolled.

4: Spectator is requested to cut paper with a pair of sharp scissors.

5: An apparent miracle is performed, as wine begins to flow.

obedient table

THIS IS ONE of the very few inexpensive stage effects that, in the hands of a clever showman, will leave a decided impression upon an audience. The magician announces that he is about to present a spiritual effect in which he will defy all laws of gravitation and prove that the power of mind over matter is stronger than generally accepted.

The magician's assistant now brings forth a table, which in size would compare favorably with the average card table. This piece of furniture is most innocent in appearance, being of the usual four-legged type, made of wood and free from drapes or fringes. Standing a few feet away from the table the magician assumes a mystic pose and rubs his hands violently. Creating as much of a picture as possible, he begins making mystic passes over the table, two legs of which seem to slowly leave the floor, and rise upward into mid-air. Slowly, the tipping of the table continues until the table stands without apparent assistance, suspended in this position, at an angle of about 45 degrees. With a wave of his hand the table sinks downward until its four legs are once more resting on the floor. This impressive experiment is several times repeated. The magician is now apparently much exhausted from the energy he has mentally employed to obtain the effect.

Now to explain how this phenomenal effect has been accomplished. A concealed off-stage assistant of natural ability supplies this spiritual effect. The thin, strong thread that did the table tipping is, of course, withdrawn prior to offering the table for inspection. The magician has but to pose as the assistant does the work. A dark backdrop and proper lighting increases the string's invisibility. ★

The magician appears to cast a "spell" over an ordinary table, causing it to move at his command.

The secret? Strong thread and a capable assistant.

it's in the pocket

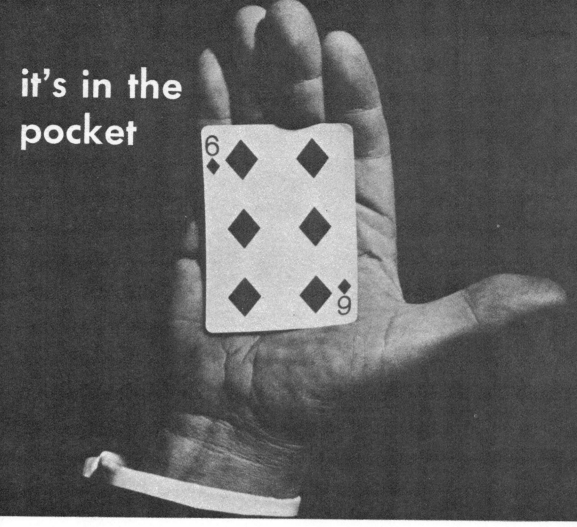

Palming a card is the talent that is very necessary to perform this trick properly; the photo shows how.

YOUR AUDIENCE will consider you extremely clever if you perform this trick effectively.

Hand a pack of cards to a person and request that he shuffle them thoroughly, think of any number between one and fifty-two, count down that number from the top of the pack and look at the card which stands at that number, square up the cards and hand them back to you. You boldly state that you will pick his card out of the fifty-two and place it in your pocket. Of course, you don't know his card, but, nevertheless, you take the bottom card from the pack in a manner that looks as if you took it from the middle of the pack, and place it in your pocket.

When the card is in your pocket you palm it and immediately place it on the top of the pack. Now in order to prove that you have his card in your pocket, you ask him at what number his card was in the pack. You now count down that number and ask him to look at the card. Of course, this is not his card, as you have placed the bottom card on the top of the pack, thus making his card stand at one card further down within the pack. Now here is where some misdirection lies: while he is looking at his card (that is not his card) you palm off the next card (which really is his card) and place it in your pocket. The party sees that you have told the truth, for the card at the number that he selected is not his and the one that he remembered is in your pocket, from whence he takes it. ★

89

magical foot

First a deck is shuffled and separated into several piles; a card is selected and placed on top of a pile.

A KICK of the deck is the novel method used in this trick to reveal a previously selected card. Without touching the cards, have someone shuffle the pack and divide it into several piles which are placed on the table. Request a spectator to select a card from the center of any pile and place it on top of one of the stacks. Have the cards piled one on top of the other, cut, squared and put on the floor. Kick the deck, and where the cards break most obviously, pick up the top card. This will be it!

Secret: Your back is to audience when a card is selected. This gives you an opportunity to take a pinch of salt from a pocket. When the pack is divided, the card chosen and placed atop any one of the piles, you point to the pile, inquiring if it is the correct one. In doing so, you drop a few grains of salt on the chosen card. When cards are piled, squared and put on the floor, all you need to do is to kick them hard, and they will separate quickly where the salt is doing its job. ★

Performer secretly drops salt (less obviously than pictured) on top of pile which holds mystery card.

When the deck is squared and placed upon the floor, performer kicks it sharply; it'll cut at the card.

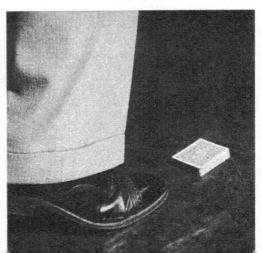

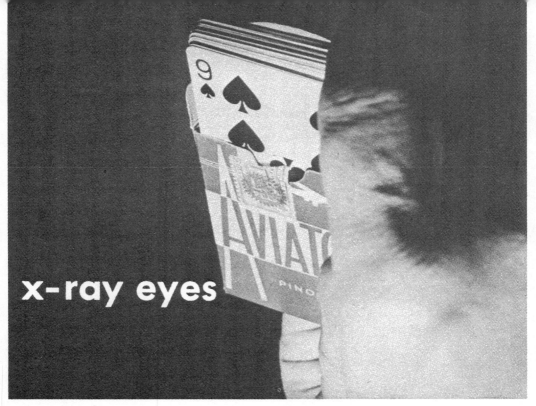

x-ray eyes

THIS IS A spectacular mental effect of the rare variety that seems absolutely convincing to an audience. The magician removes a deck of 52 cards and passes them about freely for complete inspection. When the audience is convinced of their genuineness, he requests one or more of the spectators to thoroughly shuffle the deck which, when returned to him, he replaces in the case.

Holding this case of cards at arm's length, he explains that by psychic force he will see clearly through the case and read the entire rotation of the cards. He does so.

Secret: A small section in the lower corner of the case has been cut away, enabling the entertainer to actually see the index of every card in the deck. The magician's thumb has covered this opening during the necessary handling of the deck and case. ★

With deck inserted in case, trick is to "read" cards.

This is accomplished simply; cut notch in the case.

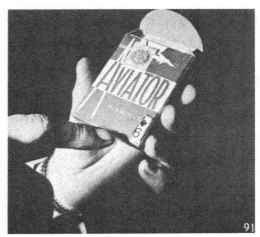

sole of the wizard

THE MAGICIAN shows a playing card which, for example, we will suppose to be the ace of spades. This is shown, both back and front, and to all appearances, seems intact. The magician now places this card face upward upon the floor, and puts his foot upon it, so that the sole of the shoe completely conceals the card from view. As the foot is lifted, an impressive transformation is observed. The card has mystically changed into the three of clubs. This card is then presented for examination.

Two cards are used to do the trick. They are firmly held together, and shown as one. Taking care not to disturb the position they are placed upon the floor, the face of the upper card uppermost. A bit of gum or wax has been previously attached to the sole of the shoe or to the surface of the ace. When the foot is placed upon the card, the sticky substance compels the card to adhere, when the foot is lifted, the top card sticks tightly to the performer's under sole and cannot be seen. ★

Left, the ace of spades is shown to the audience; above, it's placed on the floor and stepped upon.

When the foot is removed from the ace, it seems to have magically changed to the three of clubs!

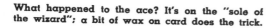

What happened to the ace? It's on the "sole of the wizard"; a bit of wax on card does the trick.

Second secret of the trick is that two cards are used instead of one—they're held firmly in hand.

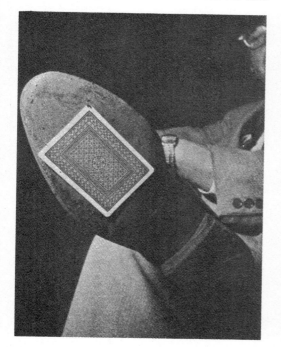

columbus outdone

A small pile of salt concealed under the tablecloth is the basis for this trick; place it unobserved.

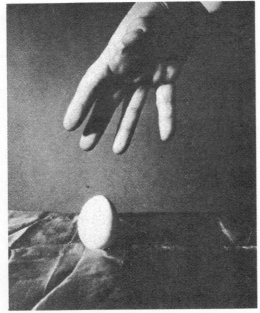

When the heavy end of the egg is carefully placed on the salt pile, it will balance as if by magic.

THE STORY has often been told of the incident in which Christopher Columbus made good his boast of being able to successfully balance an ordinary egg upon a table top. History relates that he accomplished this feat by simply cracking the lower part of the egg shell and then standing it upon the table.

In our startling experiment the magician actually accomplishes this unique feat without any injury to the egg.

To perform this effect you previously place some salt under the tablecloth. By standing the egg large end down over the salt, the egg can be made to stand upright. When friends try to duplicate the feat, they fail. Make sure that they try the effect upon some other section of the tablecloth. ★

ups and downs

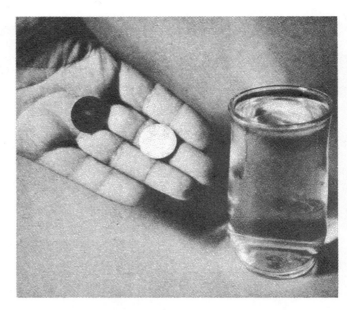

Props needed for this trick are simple: an ordinary glass of water and two discs are used. One of the discs is concealed— one is aluminum; other, zinc.

Aluminum disc is floated on water by performer.

THIS IS A TRULY fine pocket trick. The wizard passes a metal disc (about the size of a 25-cent piece) for inspection. It is then dropped into a tumbler filled with water and mysteriously floats. However, when anyone else trys it, it sinks.

You have two discs, one of aluminum, the other of zinc. They look alike. The one will float, the other will sink. After floating the aluminum disc, you wipe it with a handkerchief to dry it off and substitute it for the one of zinc concealed in the handkerchief. The zinc disc is the one your friends try to float. They, of course, find themselves unsuccessful in their attempts. ★

Palmed zinc disc is handed to a spectator, while the aluminum disc is hidden from view. In the spectator's attempt to float disc, it will sink.

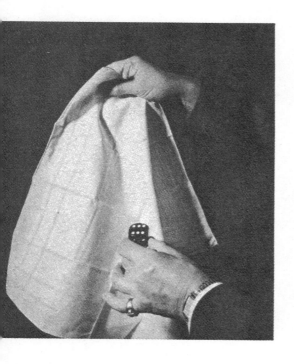

you know

the

number

Above, a die is shaken beneath a handkerchief.

Yet the performer can tell the top number! See text.

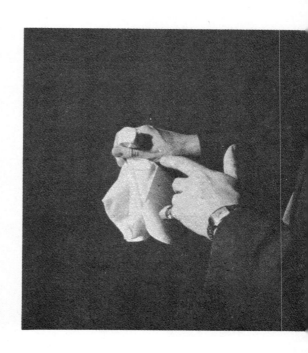

TO READ a die under a handkerchief, lay a large bone die on the palm of your hand and cover it with a white cambric or linen handkerchief. Have any one of the audience place his (or her) hand underneath the handkerchief and turn the die. You then announce to the audience the number on the die that is uppermost. Remove the handkerchief and let your guess be verified.

Secret: When you bring your hand containing the die to your forehead, wrap the handkerchief tightly across the face of the die and the spots can be plainly seen through the meshes of the handkerchief. ★

mysterious
matches

THIS MAGICAL EFFECT has the magician changing an empty book of matches into a full one. He first shows the folder empty, then closes it, makes a few passes, then open it, showing the paper full of matches.

The simple explanation is this: Before the trick the magician has pasted the black striking strip across the lower edge of a full book of matches and holds the case so as to conceal the matches. ★

An ordinary book of matches is shown to be empty.

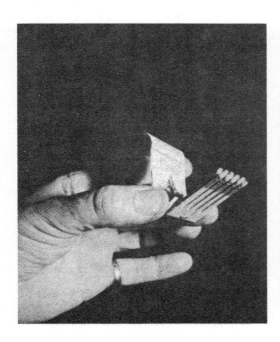

A quick flip of the wrist and the book is full!

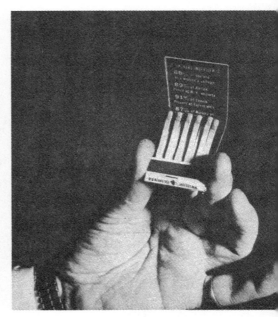

Secret of trick is a double-banded match-book.

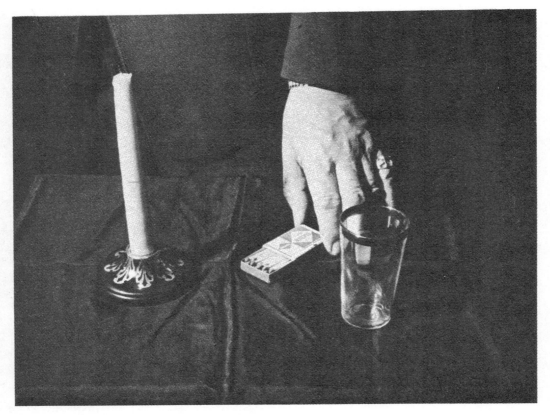

1: The performer has the props shown on his table; they include a candle, a water glass and matches.

fire magic

A number of coins are placed in rear of the open match box; when box is closed, coins fall in hand.

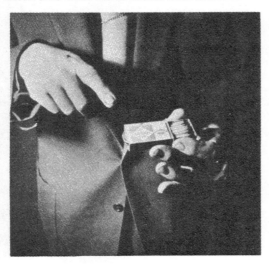

AN ORDINARY CANDLE resting in a candle stick is standing on a table. The entertainer bares his arms to the elbow and proves his hands unquestionably empty. Without false moves he reaches for a match from a match box which is also standing on the table. He lights the candle. Then, reaching into the flame for a brief moment, he mysteriously produces a handful of coins which he showers into a glass standing nearby.

To perform this effect, the only apparatus necessary is the candle, the glass, a drawer type match box, and five or six fifty-cent pieces. The coins are secretly concealed in the back section of the match box which lies half open upon the table. In the act of lighting the candle, the drawer of the box is pushed back into position, forcing a stack of coins unnoticed into the magician's hands. The rest is obvious. ★

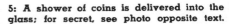

3: At this point performer can casually set box on table and switch match to left hand.

5: A shower of coins is delivered into the glass; for secret, see photo opposite text.

2: With sleeves rolled up and no false moves, the performer lights the candle.

4: With the candle lighted, magician quickly blows out the match and picks up glass.

difficult catch

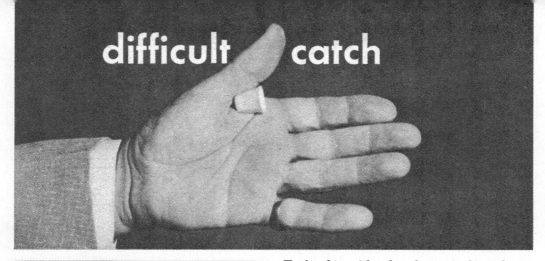

The hand is quicker than the eye in this trick; one thimble is palmed as the other is tossed in air.

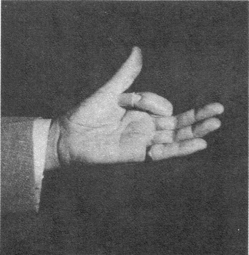

As original thimble falls, palmed one is fingered.

THIS EFFECTIVE BIT of magical jugglery makes a fine pocket trick. The magician displays and passes for inspection a bright red thimble, sufficiently large to fit over his index finger. When the thimble is returned, he tosses it into the air and, as it descends, catches it upon the index finger. He repeats the effect several times, yet always successfully.

The secret: Two identical thimbles are employed. One is palmed in the fleshy part of the hand between the thumb and the index finger. As the original thimble is tossed into the air, the magician secures the duplicate upon his finger tip and catches the other thimble as it falls. The illusion is perfect. A little practice is essential to reach perfection. ★

In a quick motion, index finger is extended as . . .

. . . falling thimble is caught and palmed as shown.

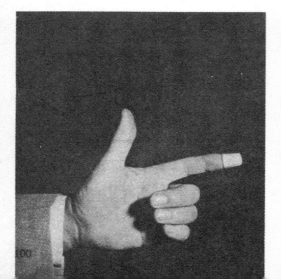

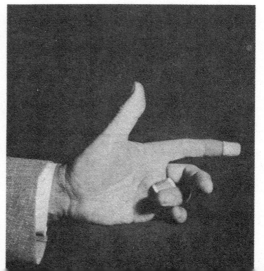

seed magic

Props needed for this trick are simple, everyday ones—ginger ale, grapes and a glass will serve.

ANYTIME YOU SEE a bunch of grapes about, you might try this one. The wizard shows an ordinary grape seed and claims that it has magical properties. He drops it in a glass filled with ginger ale, and the seed sinks to the bottom. The performer waves his hand over the glass and the seed mysteriously rises to the top. Again the magician waves his hand and the seed dips to the bottom again. This rising and falling will keep up as long as the ginger ale is "alive" and has plenty of bubbles.

Secret: The seed is too heavy to float, but the bubbles of the ginger ale are strong enough to lift the seed to the surface of the liquid a number of times. ★

Magician claims to have a "magic seed" which will rise and fall in a glass of liquid at his command.

Grape seed is dropped into a glass of ginger ale; secret is fact that carbonated bubbles lift seed.

enchanted whistle

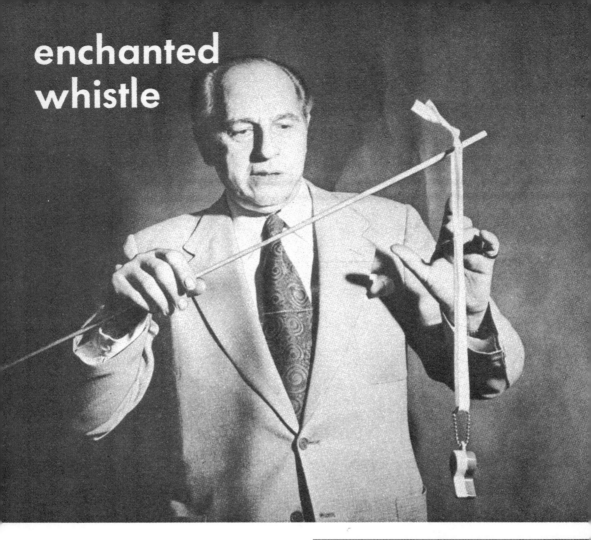

Whistle on a stick is made to mysteriously blow. Secret is a duplicate whistle and rubber bulb.

THE MAGICIAN WALKS among his audience with a stick about fourteen inches long, to the end of which an ordinary whistle has been attached to a short piece of ribbon. This simple type of apparatus bears minute inspection. At the magician's will the whistle mysteriously blows in short, sharp tones. It now can be caused to spell out the name of a playing card or whistle forth answers to questions —one for yes, and two for no.

As to the secret, a duplicate whistle is secretly concealed in the performer's sleeve. This whistle is attached to a small piece of rubber tubing and the other end to a rubber bulb. The bulb is held beneath the performer's armpit. Slight pressure will cause the whistle to blow. ★

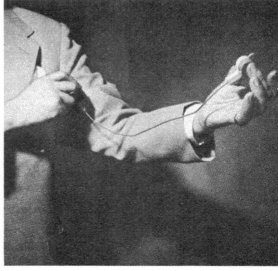

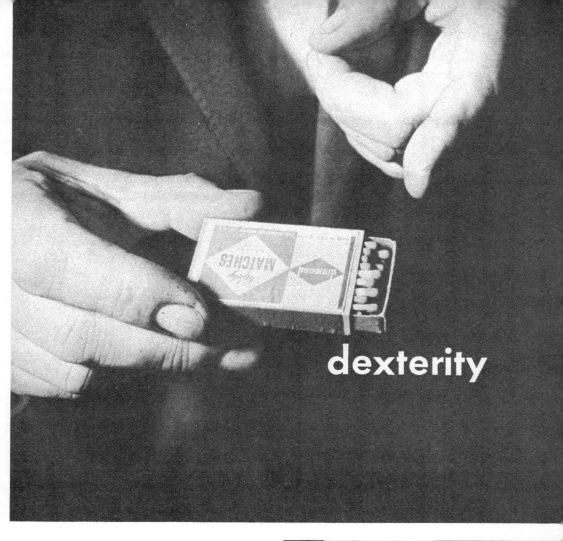

dexterity

It's possible to drop an ordinary box of matches and have the box stand on end with every drop.

Secret of this trick is to have the match box slightly open at top when dropping it; try it and see.

THIS CLEVER IMPROMPTU effect can be repeated with little fear of its secret being detected. As in many tricks of this caliber, a bit of misdirection will help considerably. Show an ordinary box of matches. Hold it about twelve inches above a table. Now drop the box. Your friends will be surprised that it stands on end. When others try it, the box will always fall over. *Secret*: Before you drop the box, open the drawer on the top side, concealing the fact that it is open with your hand. When the match box drops, the drawer shuts, balancing the box so that it stands. ★

water magic

A TRANSPARENT GLASS jar is freely examined and then filled with water. A small object such as a ring or a coin is dropped into the bowl. Baring his arm to the elbow, the wizard reaches into the water and removes the object. Upon examination of the hand and the arm, they are found to be entirely dry.

The secret is simple. At an opportune moment a small quantity of lycopodium is dusted on the water. The trick now works itself. ★

In this trick, water can be prepared beforehand to insure against a giveaway on part of performer.

Lycopodium, a powder available at most trick shops, is dusted onto water after bowl is filled.

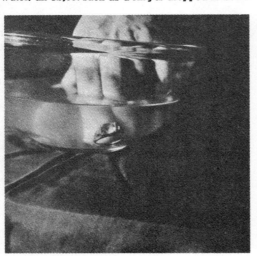

With powder secretly dusted on surface of the water, an object such as a ring is dropped in bowl.

When the magician reaches into the bowl for the object and then removes it, his hand emerges dry!

talking dime

Above, a bit of salt is secretly dropped into a cola bottle which still contains a small amount of cola.

When a coin is placed on the rim of the bottle, the gaseous action of soda will cause movement.

ALTHOUGH after-dinner tricks are numerous, one as effective and mysterious as the Talking Dime is extremely rare. The effect is as follows: the performer reaches for a common cola bottle, the contents of which have been emptied, and places the bottle upon the table several feet away from where he is seated. He requests the loan of a dime, which, when passed to him, is marked for future identification. The dime is placed upon the mouth of the bottle and the magician explains while passing his hand in mystic fashion over the affair the dime mysteriously accepts the qualities of mystic influence and thus becomes endowed with power to talk. After a few minutes have elapsed the dime is seen to mysteriously move up and down, causing distinct clinks. If the performer chooses,

he might request a spectator to suggest a small number such as eight or ten and the dime will obediently clink to the given number.

Explanation: During the festivities the magician has secretly poured a small quantity of salt into the palm of his hand. At an opportune moment, the salt is dropped inside the bottle, the bottom of which must contain a small quantity of cola. After a few moments the gas created in the bottle from this mixture will actually cause the dime to bob up and down for quite a length of time. The matter of counting a given number, or perhaps answering a question, one clink for yes, two clinks for no, is simply a matter of time control and depends upon the salesmanship of the performer. ★

the mystic deck

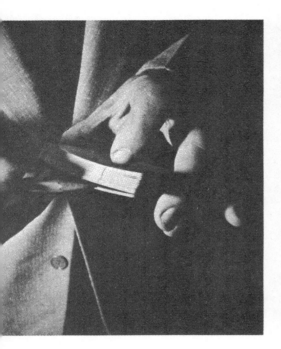

A pencil line across the side of deck is the aid.

Mystery card is determined by lack of a mark.

THIS EFFECT is done with an ordinary pack of playing cards; though very simple, it is extremely mystifying. The magician goes through his audience shuffling a pack of cards. He passes the cards from hand to hand and requests a member of the audience to select a card. Immediately after the card is returned to the deck, the magician locates the card, names it and hands it to the party who drew it. To further display his mental powers he repeats the effect, this time asking three different people to select cards, show them to their friends and then place them back into the pack proving to their satisfaction that the cards selected have been hopelessly lost in the deck. Each of these three cards, which the magician positively does not know the names of, are located in the deck and drawn out and handed back to the selectors.

This is an excellent after-dinner trick, and when properly presented leaves a marked impression on the spectators. The secret is simple but well worth while. Many times a simple trick like this one gains all kinds of credit for the magician.

Before presenting the effect, the magician has, on one side of the deck near the top, drawn a pencil line across the thickness of the pack. Only the magician knows the line is there and this side of the cards should be kept away from the audience. When the cards are selected from the pack, allow the spectators assisting to draw their cards clear of the deck, on the pretense of telling them what to do, and warning them not to allow you to see the cards, reverse the entire deck in your hands and have them immediately replace the cards drawn. Now after the proper squaring of the deck and telling them their cards are hopelessly lost, step back from the audience and turn the cards sideways in your hands holding the pencil-line side of the pack away from them. Sight the non-marked cards selected and complete the illusion. ★

demon wine glass

AN ORDINARY wine glass is passed for inspection. The glass later mysteriously fills itself with wine.

Explanation: The liquid is originally contained in a large rubber bulb which, with the assistance of a small narrow strap, is attached to the performer's upper arm so as to bring the rubber bulb between the arm and body. To the bulb is attached a tube which is carried down the performer's sleeve; to the tube metal tubing is fastened; in turn, the metal is attached to the finger. When the bulb is pressed liquid is forced into the glass. ★

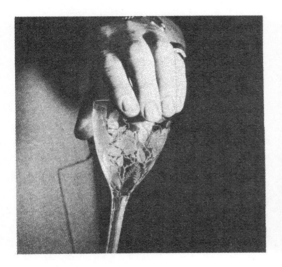

An empty glass mysteriously fills with red wine!

Rubber bulb and tube and metal clip are used.

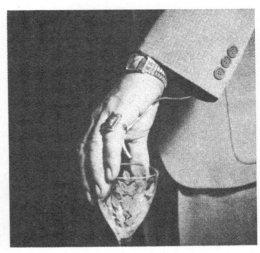

Sideview shows that apparatus is used for trick.

Glass can be mysteriously filled again and again.

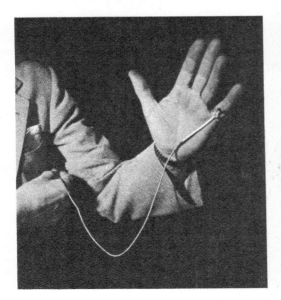

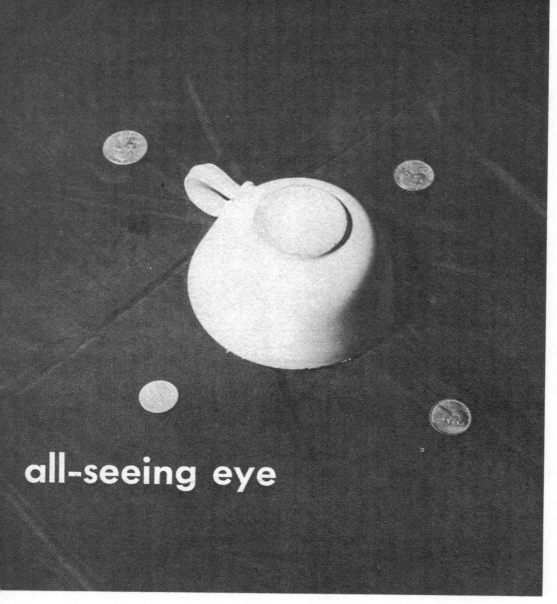

all-seeing eye

Position of cup handle (placed by assistant) denotes denomination of coin placed beneath cup.

THIS TRICK IS a bit of artful deception which has successfully mystified quite a number of professional wizards.

The performer states that he can tell the denomination of any coin placed under a cup while he is out of the room. He leaves the room and a coin is placed under a cup. The magician comes back and immediately announces the denomination of the coin.

Secret: An accomplice is used. The position of the handle of the cup as illustrated acts as the key to the denomination of the coin. Consider the dime at six o'clock, the quarter at nine o'clock, the nickel at twelve o'clock and the penny at three o'clock. Be sure your assistant does not turn the cup handle *after* he has put the cup over the coin. He simply places the cup over the coin with the hand already pointing in the proper position. ★

Any spectator cannot pick up metal with magnet.

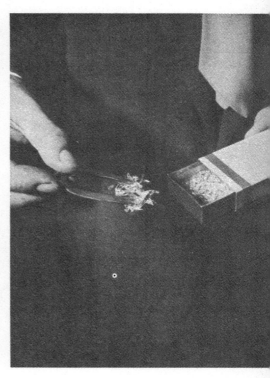

Yet the magician does the trick with no trouble!

Secret is in compartment box: zinc, steel are used.

magnetic
control

IN THIS EXPERIMENT the magician shows his audience, to their amazement, that a magnet is not always magnetic. A horseshoe magnet is passed for inspection. The performer then hands members in his audience a match box filled with metal filings. Strangely the metal filings are not attracted to the magnet. The magician then passes his hands over the steel, and plunging it into the box he causes the metal filings to adhere to it.

As to the secret of this effect, the magnet is of the ordinary variety, the match box is double. One compartment contains zinc filings, the other compartment used by the magician contains steel or iron filings. The spectators test the first section, the magician uses the second. ★

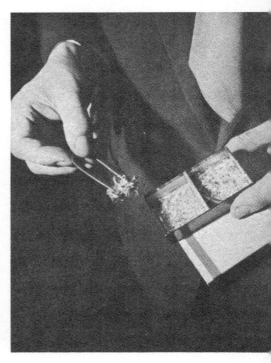

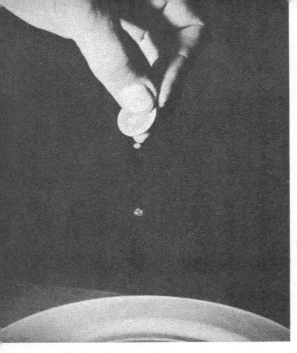

the

lady

cries

A squeezed coin is made to "cry" by the magician.

Secret of trick is a palmed piece of wet paper tissue.

Before trick is performed, magician wets paper.

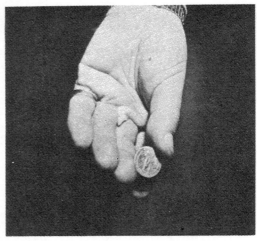

THIS IS A GENUINE magical novelty which amuses as well as mystifies. Show a 25-cent piece and point to the engraving of the liberty head. Say you are strong enough to hug her until she cries. Squeeze the coin between the fingers and real tears seem to flow.

Secret: Conceal a small ball of wet tissue paper between the first two fingers of the right hand. The coin will "cry" by simply squeezing the wet paper. ★

A playing card can be made to jump out of a water glass at the performer's command.

the
flying
card

THIS BIT OF playing card magic, like most good tricks, is simple to operate, and proves exceedingly weird in effect. The magician places an ordinary playing card into a tumbler and with a wave of his hand makes the card jump out.

Preparation: Before showing the trick, take a piece of soap and carefully sharpen it to a point. Run it up and down in delicate lines on two opposite sides inside the glass. When putting the card into the glass, make sure it's placed exactly on the soaped parts. Pressing the card down and releasing it instantly will cause it to jump up the slippery sides. If a spectator wants to imitate you, see that he puts the card in the glass on any of the unsoaped portions. The glass must be of the sloping variety. Before the trick, experiment with a few types of drinking glasses and select the one that offers the best results. ★

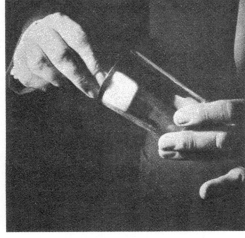

Beforehand, glass is prepared with edge of soap. If someone else attempts trick, glass is turned.

111

enchanted deck

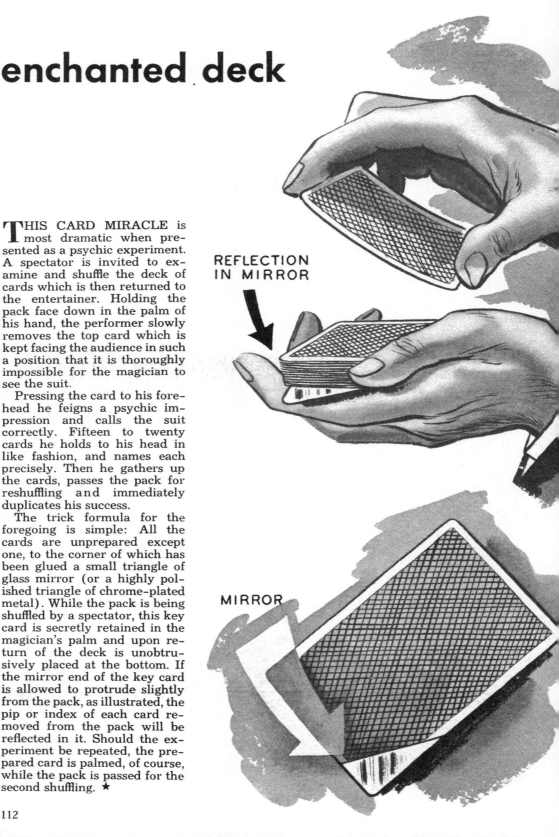

REFLECTION IN MIRROR

MIRROR

THIS CARD MIRACLE is most dramatic when presented as a psychic experiment. A spectator is invited to examine and shuffle the deck of cards which is then returned to the entertainer. Holding the pack face down in the palm of his hand, the performer slowly removes the top card which is kept facing the audience in such a position that it is thoroughly impossible for the magician to see the suit.

Pressing the card to his forehead he feigns a psychic impression and calls the suit correctly. Fifteen to twenty cards he holds to his head in like fashion, and names each precisely. Then he gathers up the cards, passes the pack for reshuffling and immediately duplicates his success.

The trick formula for the foregoing is simple: All the cards are unprepared except one, to the corner of which has been glued a small triangle of glass mirror (or a highly polished triangle of chrome-plated metal). While the pack is being shuffled by a spectator, this key card is secretly retained in the magician's palm and upon return of the deck is unobtrusively placed at the bottom. If the mirror end of the key card is allowed to protrude slightly from the pack, as illustrated, the pip or index of each card removed from the pack will be reflected in it. Should the experiment be repeated, the prepared card is palmed, of course, while the pack is passed for the second shuffling. ★

While smoking, the conjurer claims an ability to make his cigarette disappear and then return; he then does it.

elusive cigarette

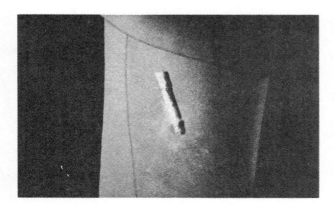

"Vanished" cigarette is actually attached to the clothing.

Empty hand is shown, then the cigarette is quickly returned.

WITH THE conjurer's sleeves bared to the elbows, and without the use of cumbersome knickknacks, the magician is able to spirit away a lighted cigarette and to reproduce it at will.

Preparing for this feat requires only a few minutes—the apparatus consists of a special small cap of cork-colored metal made to fit the tip of the cigarette thus eliminating danger of detection. Before presenting the trick, the magician secures the cap (which has a pin attached) over the cigarette. Then, stepping confidently before the audience, he lights it. Cigarette in hand, he makes a series of up and down movements, pretending to throw the cigarette in mid-air, while actually pinning it to the sides of his trousers. A few hocus-pocus gestures, and he slowly separates his fingers showing the cigarette has vanished. Repeating these movements, possession of the cigarette is regained. The intervals between disappearance and reappearance must be brief, so that the slow-burning cigarette can do no injury. ★

tell tale match

Initials can be made to appear on a match head!

THIS EFFECTIVE little pocket trick is one you will probably perform many times. The effect is startling. While a spectator holds a
lighted match and concentrates on the initials of his name, the initials
mysteriously appear on the burnt-out match head.

Secretly, learn the initials of the victim. Beforehand, using an
ordinary pencil, print the initials on the head of the match, using
heavy strokes. The match remains attached to its paper folder.

In presenting the effect you patter about mind over matter, we
have never met before, etc. Remove the pack of matches from your
pocket, tear off the proper match, light it and hand it to him. Ask him
to look into the flame and concentrate upon his initials. Request him
to blow out the flame and look carefully at the match. He will be
greatly surprised to find his initials printed there. ★

In this trick, a card is selected and identified from a deck which remains behind the performer's back!

phenomenal card trick

THIS trick should be performed with an old deck of cards, if possible. With your back to the audience, cards face down, your hands holding them behind you, you spread the cards and have someone select a card, remember it and return it to the pack. Hold the pack tightly so that he, on pushing it back, can't quite put it back all the way. Now turn around, facing the audience, the cards still behind you, and you ask for deep concentration. This is when you do your stuff.

Tear off a corner of the card that is sticking out, the corner with the symbol on it; turn that card around and replace it so that it still sticks out a bit, as before. All this time, the card corner is in your right hand. Bring your right hand to your brow, as if you are concentrating. This gives you an opportunity to see what the symbol is. You now know what the card is. You then turn around, with your back to the audience, and name the correct card. Remove the torn card first chance you get. ★

With deck behind back, Dunninger "concentrates."

Secret is bit of card torn behind back, then viewed.

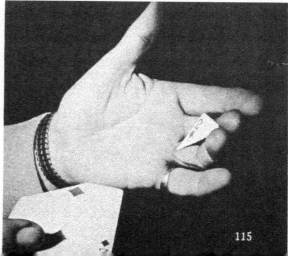

A call on a dead phone to the mysterious Cagliostro results in secret information.

the phone of cagliostro

THIS IS A NEW and absolutely original test. The proper performer, if an experienced showman, is able to create a sensation with this trick. The effect is entirely foreign from anything that has been previously demonstrated, and the trick offers an inexhaustible array of possibilities.

The magician has been demonstrating a number of tricks in magic and mind-reading, and announces that the final number of his program is a positive masterpiece of modern second-sight. He explains that for years Hindu magicians have been credited with being expert mentalists and able to send thought waves from the minds of one subject to another. This amazing test, he explains, has been presented regardless of distance and, in some cases, statistics prove that a message has been sent successfully over an area of thirty miles.

"More remarkable than that," he continues, "I will present for the first time before the American public an instrument which is acknowledged by scientists and investigators to be an unexplained phenomenon." (Brings forth a telephone.) "This instrument requires no introduction. Although it resembles a telephone similar to the one that you all have spoken into

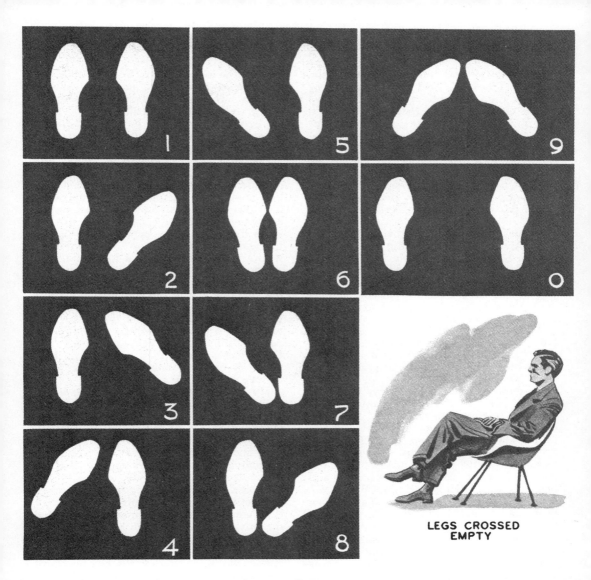

Secret of imparted information from departed Cagliostro is in assistant's maneuvers with feet.

daily, it differs greatly in one remarkable respect. As you see, it has absolutely no wire connection, yet, with it, I can speak to departed spirits. I do not mean that any of you ladies or gentlemen could use this as an instrument of conversation with any of your dear ones that might have passed across the borderline. This phone you see is a direct wire to Cagliostro.

"For the benefit of those who may not recognize this name, Cagliostro was a learned scholar of black-art and witchcraft who died several centuries ago. The old fellow, however, has never been silenced and still keeps in touch with the modern

world. In fact, I am in daily communication with any fellow wizard of the other land, and in my various chats with him tell him all that transpires here. I tell him all about our greatest events, keep him posted upon all sports; in short he knows all about the doings on this earth. But he is by no means an ungrateful fellow, and in return for the information I give him, he often tells me things about you and your doings. I see you smiling as if you were in doubt as to the truth of my assertion.

"If you will permit me, I will demonstrate that you can't do anything while my back is turned that good old Cagliostro would not see and tell me about for the asking. I have a steel chest, and a key that fits the lock, both of which I implore you to examine." The entertainer takes a box from the table and passes it for inspection. This is found to be made of sheet iron, firmly riveted, of massive construction and impressively secure. A strong Yale lock built into the box secures the lid firmly when the key is turned. This box is as exactly as it appears. It is in no way prepared, there are no secret panels or slides.

"Now," the magician continues, "I will leave the room and during my absence someone in my audience be good enough to take an object and put it in this chest. Lock the box, in which condition you are assured I cannot possibly tell its contents and place the chest upon the table, alongside of the telephone."

After the magician leaves the room some lady, we will say, takes a small hand mirror out of her purse, and secretes it inside the box which is then locked and placed upon the table.

Re-enter the performer. "My friends, I believe you are completely assured that there is no one with an X-ray eye sufficiently powerful to pierce the metal cover of the box and see its contents. I will call up my old mystic friend, who has been watching all the while and who will tell me all about it." He lifts the receiver and begins to talk. "Hello! Hello! Well, well, it is good to hear your voice again. How is my old friend Cagliostro . . . well, and happy as ever . . . that is surely pleasing to know. . . . I have a question I would like to ask you . . . what's that . . . you know all about it . . . oh, you do know the question . . . and you also know where I am . . . yes, indeed, I am interested in the contents of the box . . . what's that you say. . . . 'A lady's small hand mirror' . . . oh, it is . . . thank you, professor. . . . I will hang up for the present, but call you back shortly. . . . I have a few skeptics present who are doubtful of your ability . . . thank you ever so much . . . goodbye for the moment."

The performer hangs up the receiver and opens the box. Removing the mirror, he returns it to the owner. After the applause has subsided, the magician offers to repeat the experiment. He again leaves the room, and during his absence another article is locked into the box. The magician returns, and once more rings up Cagliostro who without difficulty again analyzes the contents of the locked chest. Several times the experiment is repeated and always with success. This is little short of miraculous. Some well-posted entertainers and exponents of the mystic art have found themselves at an absolute loss for a practical solution.

The trick, rather difficult as it may appear, is comparatively simple. It requires considerable practice before a demonstration should be attempted. The magician has a secret understanding with an assistant who sits among the spectators. He has studied a silent code, by which he signals the necessary information to the wonderworker. So natural is this form of transmission that it will deceive the cleverest observer. This confederate, apparently an inactive member of the audience has a pair of restless tell-tale feet. By the way his feet are resting upon the floor, together with the manner in which his toes are pointed, the magician is at once able to tell the object secreted in the box. The language of the feet, conveys a number code as seen in the illustration.

My readers will conceive that the silent assistant can transmit any number to the magician by the language of the feet. A chart which has been previously memorized by both is not only prepared in rotation, but must be arranged with a number arrangement as well. A sample chart is shown.

Should a joker, often found in a crowd, suggest that the box be left empty to trick the magician, our performer has provided for this probability by an additional sign. The silent confederate has but to cross his feet, which is an indication of an empty chest. Should an item in the box be plural the assistant plays with his watch-chain or tie in addition to the foot language. For instance, should the magician by looking at the assistant's feet find them to be in position 5, he at once knows that a cigarette has been locked in the box. Should he observe that the confederate is likewise also playing with his watch-chain he at once knows that they are plural and Cagliostro informs him that cigarettes have been placed in the box. This idea is carried out with other objects as well.

As considerable time is consumed during the magician's imaginary conversation with the voice over the telephone, the confederate has sufficient time to give him the desired code. If the movement of the feet are made quite slowly, they will not become conspicuous. ★

NUMERICAL KEY

No. 1 — A finger ring
No. 2 — A handkerchief
No. 3 — A lady's watch
No. 4 — A gentleman's watch
No. 5 — A cigarette
No. 6 — A cigarette case
No. 7 — A cigar
No. 8 — A cigar-case
No. 9 — A pencil
No. 10 — A pen
No. 11 — A visiting-card
No. 12 — A card-case
No. 13 — A playing card
No. 14 — A playing card case

No. 15 — A necklace
No. 16 — A bracelet
No. 17 — A stick-pin
No. 18 — A watch chain
No. 19 — A vanity box
No. 20 — A lipstick
No. 21 — A powder puff
No. 22 — Keys
No. 23 — Key-ring
No. 24 — Eye-glasses
No. 25 — Eye-glass case
No. 26 — A letter
No. 27 — A wallet
No. 28 — A coin

No. 29 — A check
No. 30 — A bill
No. 31 — A book
No. 32 — A match
No. 33 — A box of matches or match box
No. 34 — A tooth-pick
No. 35 — A collar button
No. 36 — A note
No. 37 — A piece of string
No. 38 — A flask
No. 39 — An emblem of some order
No. 40 — A flower

What passes for a "ghost" drawing music from a violin is actually an assistant who, unseen, pulls on string.

ghostly music

SO-CALLED spiritualistic effects are always of interest. Many are the tricks of the fraudulent mediums.

In my travels I have been present at sittings given by the best of them and have sat and held hands in the circles of the worst of them. They are all of one ilk. The cleverest are but little better than the crudest. Not so long ago I demonstrated to members of the New York press, at a seance held in the office of an important science magazine, that all the main tricks of the mediums can easily be duplicated. I attended a seance several weeks thereafter in which the following trick was used to convince the believers.

A plain wooden table was standing in a small bare room. An old violin was handed around for inspection and was placed near the center of the table. We were now ushered to another part of the room where we were to listen for the manifestations of musical spirits. Listening carefully, we soon heard strains of ghostly music. The ghostly strain seemed to impress the followers of the medium greatly.

On word from the medium, a number of us rushed to the table, but a quick glance convinced me that the violin had not been disturbed from its resting place. As far as "spirits" having played that was laughable. Now let me tell you how to get ghostly music.

Any kind of string instrument will do for this experiment, but a violin will be most suitable. Secure also a well-resined thread. On one end of the thread tie a small lead weight just heavy enough to allow it to be easily raised by the thread when pulled by the hand of a hidden assistant. The weight must carry the thread downward and across the strings of the violin without moving the violin from its resting place.

The end of the thread is carried across the room to a doorway opposite and then through the keyhole of this door. Upon entering the room the weighted end is secretly held in the hand of the medium. He is the last to leave the room, and during his brief stay places the thread across the strings of the violin.

When all have retired to the far end of the room and are intently listening, the assistant, who has watched the proceedings through the keyhole, slowly draws up the string and gradually lowers it. This is what causes the ghostly hands to mysteriously swing a soft bow lightly across the strings. Upon returning to the table secretly the medium gets the weight out of the way, tearing it away from the thread. The thread is pulled away through the keyhole by the concealed assistant. ★

A pair of trick handcuffs is the secret of this escape mystery.

mysterious handcuffs

THE trick handcuffs herein explained may be used in many tricks. They can also be used as a straight handcuff escape or used in a seance, as follows:

The curtain rises disclosing a stage with a cabinet made of wooden or iron standards and three sides of dark curtain material. The front of the cabinet has the drapes divided into two parts so that the entrance to the cabinet can be made by the entertainer.

A committee is called upon the stage and asked to place the handcuffs on the performer's wrists. This done, they are securely locked and the locks sealed. The key is placed in the keeping of one of the voluntary assistants. The performer now enters the cabinet and an assistant or someone from the voluntary assistants closes the curtains. The assistant borrows a coat from one of the committee and tosses it over the top of the cabinet. The cabinet top is not covered. Almost immediately the per-

former's coat flies over the top of the cabinet and he emerges wearing the coat of the gentleman. Upon examination the handcuffs are still locked.

The magician once more goes into the cabinet and in a second emerges this time with the cuffs in his hands. The method of doing this effect is this. The handcuffs are faked near one of the circlets that go over the wrist. This is a piece of bar with a socket-like arrangement with a slight projection at either side. When this socket is pressed home and a slight turn is made the cuff is locked and all looks fair, but a slight twist of this faked part allows the circlet to separate itself from the chain of the cuff. This is a very useful piece of utility apparatus and can be used in many effects necessitating the handcuffing of the performer. The cuff is opened with duplicate key inside the cabinet, if a complete release is desired. ★

pocket magic

THIS IS AN effective trick which, in spite of its simplicity, is startling in effect. The magician shuffles a deck and places it in his inside pocket. He claims he can remove a number of cards and call their suit by his sense of touch.

He calls out the four of clubs and, reaching into his pocket, draws forth the correct card. He repeats this four or five times, naming each card correctly before he produces it. His pocket can be shown empty before and after the trick.

Secret: The magician has previously removed five or six cards and memorized their names and the order in which they lay. These have been placed in the upper pocket of his vest on his right side. Therefore the coat pocket can be shown empty before he begins. Obviously the cards, as named, are drawn from the vest pocket and not from the coat pocket which contains the deck. To all appearances, as far as the spectators are concerned, the cards come from the same pocket in which the shuffled pack was visibly placed. ★

The right cards hidden in the wrong pocket is trick's secret.

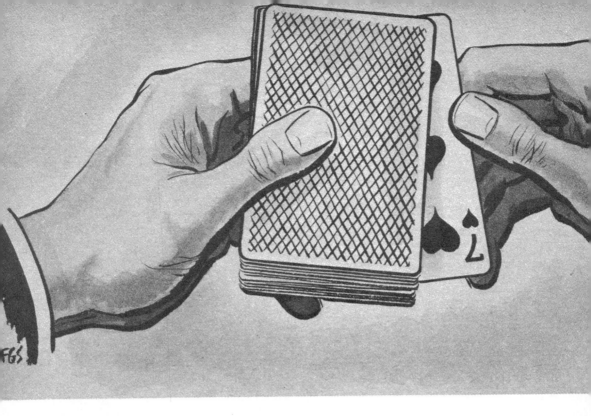

the phantom

It's possible to make fresh ink disappear entirely!

FORTUNATELY the unexpected is expected from magicians. For this reason the following effect seems little short of miraculous to an audience.

A guest quite often has occasion to jot down a note or write a letter. His mystic host directs him to his writing desk, and asks him to make himself quite at home. Pen and ink, paper, envelopes, a blotter or two, are all at his finger tips.

Unconcerned, the magician at once steps aside as his guest uncorks the ink bottle and at once begins to write. After several sentences have been written, the victim blots his script in the usual way and, to his amazement, the writing disappears.

Yes, as you may have guessed, the trick is in the blotter, which has been prepared beforehand in the following manner: The blotter has been dipped in a solution of oxalic acid and permitted to dry, then several more like applications of the acid are made. A blotter so treated will remove fresh ink completely when applied. ★

tipsy card trick

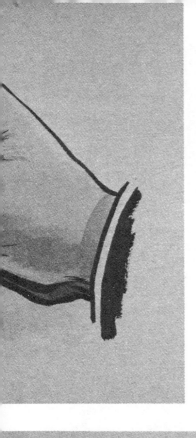

IT IS DIFFICULT to find a card trick as effective as this one, which requires as little preparation or dexterity.

Have anyone shuffle a pack of cards. Have someone else withdraw a card and look at it. The performer takes the deck from the one who shuffled it. The card is replaced in the pack and, miraculously, the selected card seems to have reversed itself.

Secret: Everything is fair until performer takes the pack back. As he does this, he secretly reverses the bottom card. When selected card is pushed back in pack, actually all the cards are face down except the bottom one which is face up, giving the illusion that all cards face one way. ★

A simple switch of the bottom card is trick's secret.

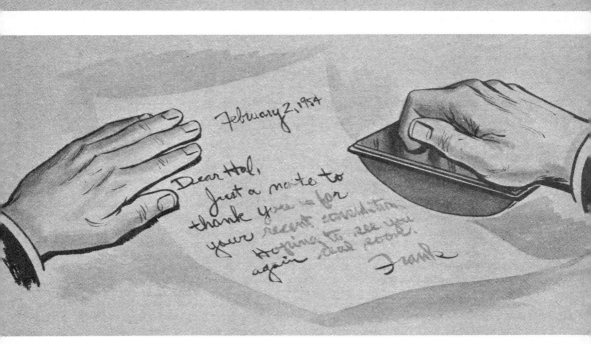

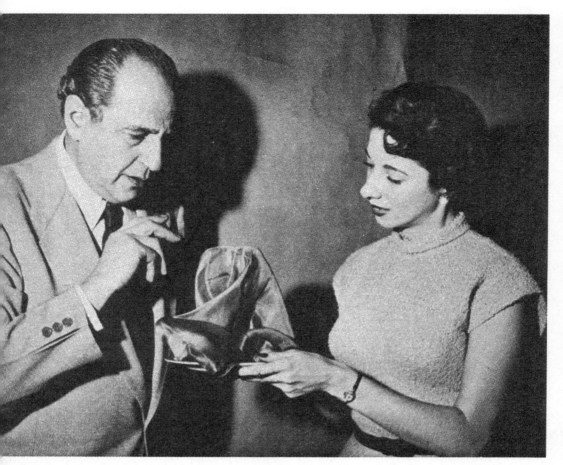

Result of this trick is to apparently change the suit of a card while it remains untouched in a water glass!

unique effect

THIS TRICK HAS a startling climax. After choosing a card, which is returned to the pack, a spectator writes its name on a slip of paper. The performer then removes a card from the pack, which spectator agrees is not his card, and this card is placed face toward the audience in a tumbler, then covered with a handkerchief. Asking a third party to read out the name on the slip, the tumbler is uncovered and there is the very card the spectator chose.

Method: A double-faced card is second from the bottom of the pack. The duplicate of the face-up side is "forced" on the spectator (see page 30) and returned to the pack. The original of the face-down side is previously removed from the pack. The assistant writes down name of card selected, and hands this slip to someone else.

Cut at the returned card and false-shuffle, but guard against the face of the fake card showing among the backs of the other cards. At the conclusion see to it that you have the double facer somewhere near the middle of the pack and the selected card on top. Fan the cards, faces to the audience, keeping the chosen card out of sight, and remove the double-facer, stating that "any card will do"—and asking "This is not the card you chose, sir, is it?"

Place this card in a tumbler, which you hold up as you cover with a handkerchief. As soon as the tumbler is covered give it a casual half-turn from the wrist, bringing the face of the selected card toward the audience. The rest is straightforward, but you can get a lot of appreciation for this number if you put it over well. ★

To the audience, the card in the glass is a deuce.

As glass is being covered with silk, glass is turned.

Card the audience now sees is a three of diamonds.

Secret of the trick is a fake card—two are glued.

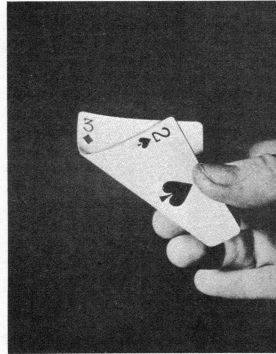

The glass mysteriously balances on a table with no visible means of support. For added effect, pour in water.

balancing glass trick

Secret can go undiscovered by spectators; it's a match under tablecloth with pull-thread attached.

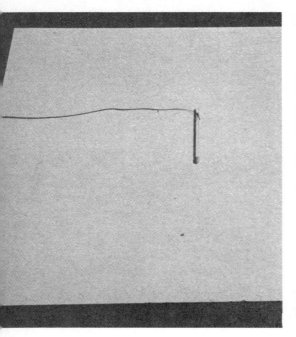

THIS after-dinner experiment has a most mystifying effect; the original trick has been improved upon by the author to make it even more mysterious to the onlookers.

A drinking glass, half-full of liquid, is placed upon the dinner table at an angle, and after a minute or two of dexterous balancing, the magician removes his fingers and the glass is seen to remain standing upon its edge, mystically balanced at an almost impossible angle.

Before presenting this effect, the magician has secretly placed a wooden match stick (of the square variety, with head broken off) beneath the tablecloth. This acts as a wedge against which the edge of the glass rests. The writer's improvement consists of a fine silk thread tied to the end of the match; the free end of the thread hangs beneath the tablecloth. After presenting the trick, one can easily pull the match away from beneath the cloth, permitting it to drop to the floor. This action can easily be executed without detection, while the magician is still seated at the table, doing the trick. Thus, many who know the method will be doubly mystified when they look beneath the cloth and find no matchstick there. ★

penetration

Below, secret of trick is duplicate coin in glass rim.

Above, dropped coin nudges another into glass.

Below, "empty" hat has original coin in the band.

Glass and hat can be shown to skeptical audience.

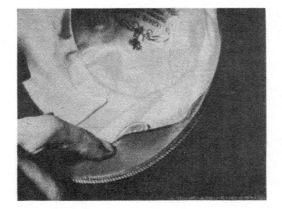

NO SPECIAL APPARATUS is required for this trick. If a little practice is employed it becomes a highly effective magical novelty.

Place a hat on a glass. Drop a quarter into the hat. It apparently goes through the crown of the hat and then drops into the glass. The hat is now shown empty. *Secret*: You use two quarters, placing one out of sight on the edge of the glass as shown in the illustration. When you drop the other coin (the only one the audience sees) into the hat, it upsets the balance of the hidden coin so it drops in the glass. Now secretly slide the coin left in the hat underneath the band so you can show hat is "empty." ★

magical magnetism

THIS is an interesting little parlor trick which may be performed around the dinner table. The amateur picks up an object, rubs it briskly on the palm of his hand and then suspends it from his finger tips, from the palm or from the back of the hand in a very mysterious manner. A very weak solution of Seccotine and water is applied to the palms and fingers and allowed to dry. This is sticky enough to cause a knife to stay in any prescribed position.

Seccotine, a special type of glue, is available in the five and dime store, usually. Should the reader have difficulty securing Seccotine, it is suggested you use any of the dental powders available in drugstores. Wernet's Powder is good for this purpose. This powder is commonly used for keeping false dentures in place. It should be applied to the hands without the use of water for the purpose of this trick. ★

Innumerable objects can be made to hold to the hand as if glued. The secret? They are glued.

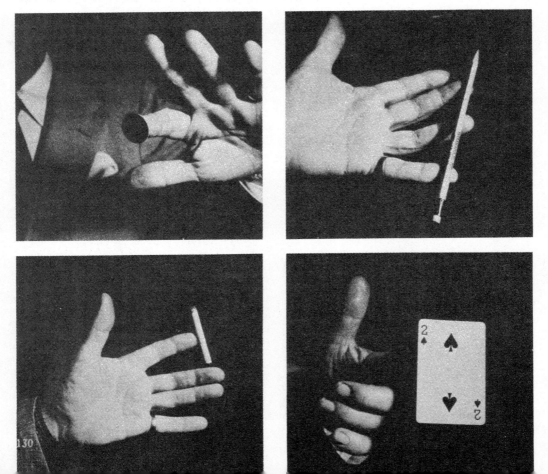

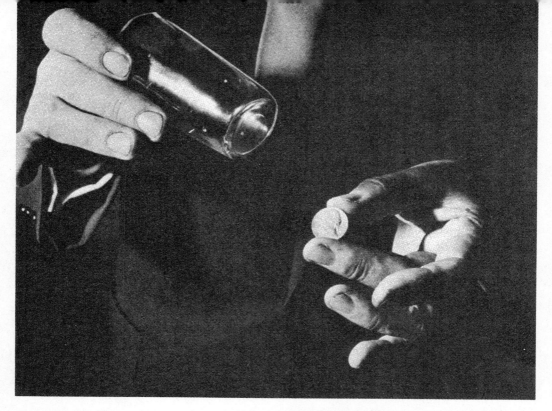

Balancing a water glass on a nickel may look easy, but it isn't unless the performer knows the secret.

it can
be done

ALTHOUGH not strictly an experiment in conjuring, this was one of Houdini's favorite after dinner tricks. An ordinary water glass empty or half-full of water can be made to balance on a nickel. *Here's the secret:* Look at the head side of the nickel carefully (Buffalo nickel preferred) and note the spot where the nose runs to the forehead. This spot makes a groove in which the edge of the glass will fit. This is a fine trick when properly performed. ★

ghost

in

the

dark

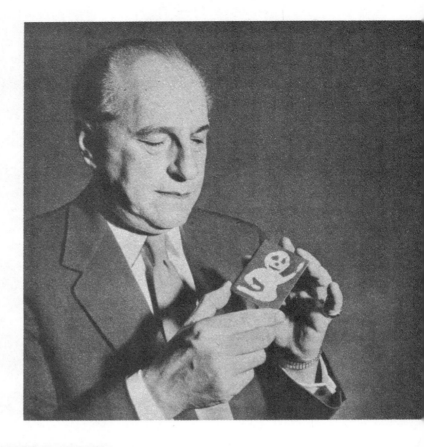

Ghost figure is painted on card with luminous paint.

During seance in dark room, the card "dances."

YOU and a group of spectators sit in a circle and hold hands. The lights are turned out leaving the room in pitch darkness. After a time a small spooky figure appears in the darkness, floating about mysteriously in the center of the circle. Of course, you are suspected of trickery, yet your group will be unable to discover the secret. You may be closely examined.

A small spooky figure is painted upon a small piece of black cardboard with luminous paint. This is held before a strong electric light for a short time before the seance starts and is then pasted to the bottom of your shoe on the instep next to the heel. Now you are set for the trick.

In the darkness you extend your leg, holding it high in mid-air and by waving your foot about from side to side, and up and down, the mystic figure appears to be floating about in the center of the circle in weird fashion. ★

color magic

Spectator inserts a color block from palette in a matchbox while performer is out of the room; when performer comes back into room, he can "divine" which color is hidden in box.

Concealed, block is scratched, then nail is viewed.

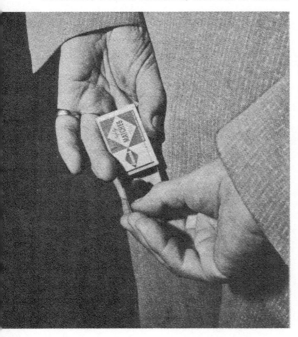

THIS is a novel and effective thought-reading trick. A painter's palette, with a number of small squares of paint of assorted colors, is passed for inspection. A small ordinary matchbox, slightly larger than the squares of paints, is likewise examined. As these articles are actually unprepared, rigid inspection is invited. During the wizard's absence from the room, one of the spectators is requested to place one of the paints in the box. Upon the magician's return, he is handed the box, which he holds behind his back in the one hand, while he raises his other hand to his head to enact a picture of deep concentration. Shortly he calls the color of the paint concealed in the box.

Secret: In the act of holding the box behind his back, the wizard quickly opens it for a moment and secures a few grains of the paint beneath his fingernail by scratching the nail across the surface of the square. In the act of raising his hand to his head, he thus has but to secretly observe the color beneath his nail. ★

mystic dice prediction

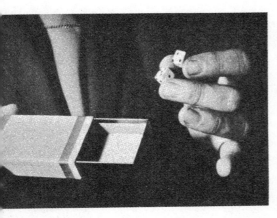

A pair of dice and empty box are shown audience.

THIS POCKET TRICK is an extremely clever deception. All that you require for the trick is a match box, some dice, a piece of paper and a pencil. With the pencil you write a prediction, fold it, and hand it to a spectator, requesting that he hold it in full view of the audience.

Show an ordinary match box and a pair of dice. The spectator puts the dice into the box and closes it. At your request, he shakes the box thoroughly. You now open the box and show him the dice. He adds the spots on the upmost sides. The prediction paper is opened, and to the amazement of the audience they find the exact total of the dice written thereupon.

The secret: Four fairly small dice are needed. Two of them have been glued to the bottom of the match box draw, near one end. The total of these, known to you beforehand, you write upon the paper. When you show the box to the spectators, you keep the part closed that contains the dice. He drops the other dice into the box, shuts the draw and shakes them. When you open the box you tilt it so that the loose dice *slide to the closed end* of the box. Let him add the total of the glued dice, and you have accomplished your miracle. ★

Dice are enclosed in box, and box is shaken up.

Magician predicts number which will show on dice.　　　Secret is simple—two pairs are used, one is glued.

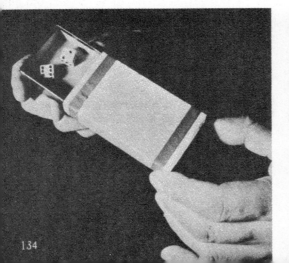

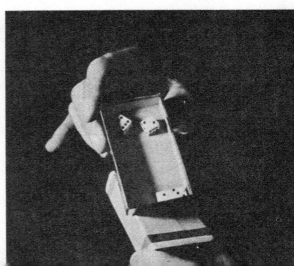

mystic jugglery

MYSTIC JUGGLERY of a decidedly mystifying nature plays the master part in this trick. The magician borrows a half-dollar from any member of the audience. This may, if desired, be marked for future record. He next presents a common table knife, which he passes for inspection. The knife, upon its return to the magician, is held in a horizontal position. The magician now proceeds to balance the coin on its edge upon the edge of the table knife. He further induces the coin to roll to and fro freely upon the edge of the knife. The procedure is exercised several times. The knife is again passed for inspection and the marked coin returned to the owner.

To accomplish this feat, the magician must provide himself with a disk, slightly smaller than the half-dollar used. Upon this disk is affixed another disk still smaller in size. Upon the free surface of this smaller disk, a small quantity of adhesive wax has been smeared.

The disk is palmed beforehand. The coin is borrowed, and the disk secretly affixed to the coin. This forms a groove, through which the blade of the knife will fit conveniently, making the rolling of the coin a simple matter, requiring little practice. The disk is detached and secretly retained in the magician's hand, when the money is returned to its owner. The knife requires no special preparation. ★

The trick below is accomplished with these props.

Coin seems to balance on edge of knife; actually, a pair of disks and a bit of wax are trick's secret.

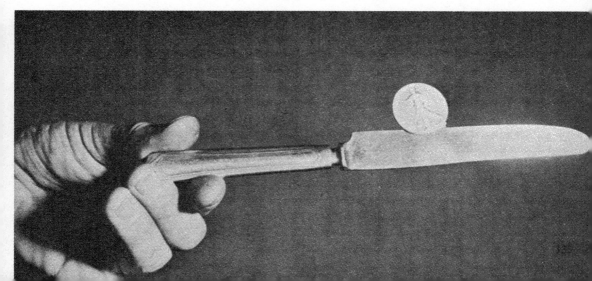

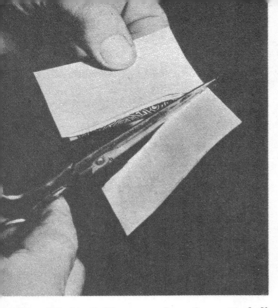

A card is inserted in an envelope, then cut in half.

Though the envelope is cut, the card remains intact!

cut and restored card

IN THIS UNUSUAL and mystifying trick the magician amazes his audience by producing a whole card from one which he has cut in half.

An ordinary brown Manila envelope just large enough to hold a playing card, a card, and a pair of scissors are the only props necessary. The performer permits any member of his audience to freely select a card from a deck of cards. This is then initialed by the spectator and visibly placed into an envelope and sealed. Holding the

envelope in one hand and the scissors in the other, the magician then cuts the envelope in half. Picking up the envelope pieces, he holds them together, tears open the seal, and withdraws the playing card intact.

Only the magician knows that the envelope has been previously prepared with a slit cut crosswise into the back. When inserting the card, it is made to project through this opening, and is bent over upon itself before the cutting operation. ★

Secret is a prepared envelope, razor slit in the back.

When cutting operation proceeds, card is bent over.

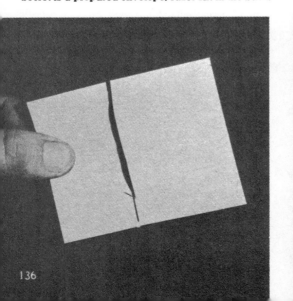

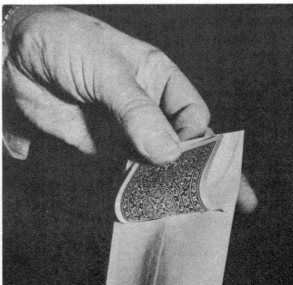

Floating ball is made of styrofoam, obtainable at any florist shop; from distance, thread is invisible.

floating ball

HERE, a styrofoam ball seemingly obeys every command of the magician's hands. This spectacular mystifying effect is done like this: A styrofoam or wooden croquet ball has a small hole drilled through it, through which a fine, strong thread passes. This thread is free at one end and is opened in the form of a loop at the other and again affixed to the ball itself. The performer on picking up the ball, passes his right hand through the loop and affixes the other end of the thread to his left hand. By bringing the hands apart, the ball may be made to rise and again on bringing them closer together the ball will be found to settle into the left hand.

At a short distance the thread will remain invisible. If the magician wears a dark suit, he is assured of greater protection against detection. When properly presented, the mysteriously floating ball proves extremely mystifying. ★

As shown, the right hand holds loop part of thread; manipulation of the loop causes ball's rise and fall.

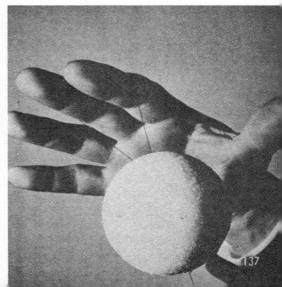

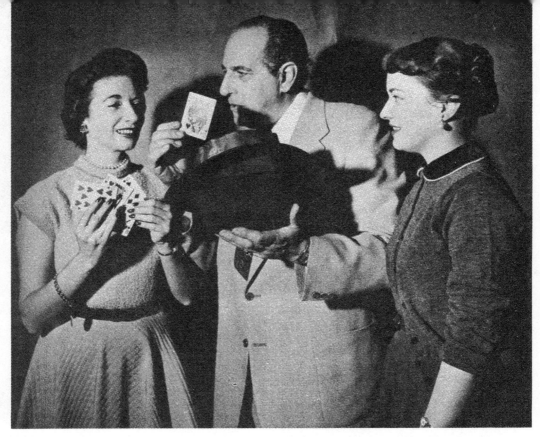

The performer reads cards before drawing them out!

card and hat trick

ALTHOUGH the explanation is simple, this card trick has proven truly mystifying to many.

The effect can be repeated as often as desired. The magician asks someone to pick three or more cards out of a deck at random, and drop these cards into a hat. Lifting the leather sweatband to "prevent his viewing" the contents of the hat, the magician raises the hat above the level of his eyes and then, as if looking through it, names the cards and in turn produces them one by one in the order named. The secret lies in the fact that a small hole has been cut in the hat, so that it will be covered by the sweatband on the inside, and the ribbon on the outside. The ribbon is pushed away by the thumb, and the magician actually looks through the hole in the hat and names the cards as he reads them. ★

Secret of trick is a hole made in hat under the band.

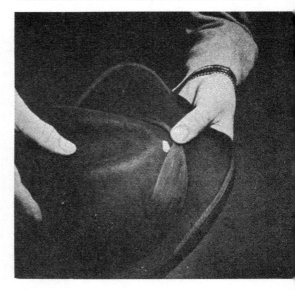

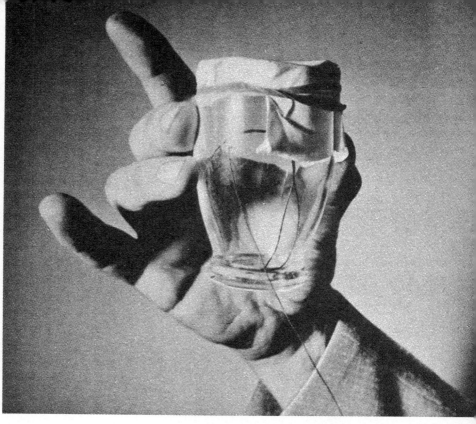

Glass on table is thought to "clink" a message when coin is dropped into it; duplicate does it.

money talks

Pocketed duplicate has coin attached to thread which is drawn through hole; pull produces "clink."

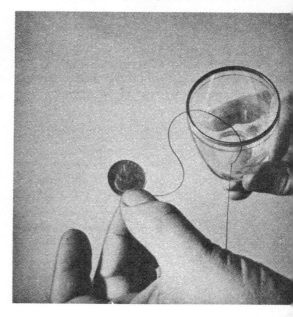

HARRY HOUDINI often employed this mystifier. A coin is examined, marked and dropped into a glass which is placed by the spectator on table. A handkerchief is then borrowed and used to cover the glass. Any questions now asked are answered by clinks of the coin. At any moment the coin can be examined.

Secret: All of the paraphernalia on the table is absolutely innocent of deception. The performer has prepared himself by placing a small duplicate tumbler in his hip pocket. This contains a coin attached to a thin thread which runs down his sleeve and is fastened at the vest. By secretly moving the string the duplicate coin in the pocket is made to produce the sound. ★

get-together card trick

If these two sets of cards are flashed quickly and separately, they will appear as same cards.

HERE'S a corker, but it must be performed quickly. Flash two cards, the nine of spades and the ten of clubs. Push these two cards into the center of the deck. Ask for someone's handkerchief. Spread the handkerchief on the table, and put the deck in the center of it. Tie the ends of the kerchief diagonally, then again. Now ask one of your bystanders to blow hard on it.

On opening the handkerchief, the two cards apparently have moved from the center of the deck to the bottom. This one defies detection unless you know the secret. Please read on.

The mystery of this trick lies in observation. When you start to perform this illusion, you have planted, unknown to your audience, the nine of clubs and the ten of spades at the bottom of the deck. If you seem casual about flashing the two cards, no one will ever notice that the cards at the bottom really aren't the same ones at all. The reason for the handkerchief routine is to confuse them. It's the spectators' poor power of observation which makes this trick possible. ★

floating
paper
ball

Levitation is an ever-popular trick; can you solve the mystery of this one by the photograph?

THE trick of levitating an object seems extremely popular with the average audience. Any effect of aerial suspension has a mystification all its own.

In this version of the trick, the performer tightly crumbles a section of a newspaper into a ball, and after mysteriously suspending it in mid-air, freely passes a solid hoop to and fro over the floating paper ball. Both paper ball and hoop are passed for inspection after the presentation.

The wizard has secretly provided himself with a length of fine silk thread about 20 inches long. The one end is looped with a small loop which fits over the finger tip, the other end of the thread with a loop to fit over the ear. The hoop which is unprepared is worn around the neck, and the thread loop in position over the ear. The paper ball is crumbled in a fashion to entwine the center of the silk thread. The illustration shows the manner in which the levitation is accomplished. The hoop lifted from the neck can be freely passed over the suspended paper ball. The trick should be performed at a fair distance from the audience to render the silk thread invisible to the spectators. ★

The performer pinpoints a card from among 52 others while the deck is under a newspaper!

devil's sight

THIS extremely effective card trick smacks of professional magic. It is sensationally effective.

Requirements: An ordinary newspaper, an ordinary pack of cards, a duplicate (the nine of hearts), a rubber band (small), and the ability to force a card.

Preparation: The newspaper lies on a table. The pack is on the table also (backs upward), with the nine of hearts at the bottom. The duplicate nine of hearts and the rubber band are placed in one of the performer's pockets.

Presentation: The performer begins: "Ladies and gentlemen, in order to present one of the most baffling tricks of the age, I would like to have a card selected." While saying this he picks up the pack from the table, but in following manner: take the upper half and place it in the left hand, backs up; then the remaining half, and place this on the top, inserting the small finger of the left hand between, so as to divide the halves. The idea of this is to bring the nine of hearts to the center of

the pack with the small finger directly beneath it. The nine of hearts is now forced (see page 30). Pack is then given to anybody, with the request to receive the selected card, to thoroughly mix it in the pack, to spread out the cards (face downward on the floor), and to again mix them.

Performer states: "In order to make it an impossibility to get the least idea as to the name or position of the selected card, I will leave the room and return when all are satisfied that the cards are well mixed." While gone he takes the duplicate Nine of Hearts and the rubber band from his pocket, places the back of the card against the sole of his right shoe, and with the rubber band holds it there. The band goes completely round the fore end of the shoe. Walking with the card attached is a simple matter as long as the performer does not slide his feet. Don't do any more walking than is necessary. Upon returning take the newspaper and offer it for examination. When all are satisfied as to the newspaper being ordinary, proceed to cover the cards

142

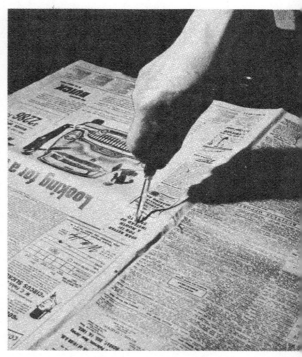

After performer forces a particular card, he leaves room while it's being shuffled back into the deck.

While out he rubber-bands a duplicate to his sole, then in arranging deck under paper, slips it off.

in the following manner: stand behind the mixed cards, open the newspaper to its widest and hold it with the two hands at one end. The other end should touch the floor so as to hide the lower half of the performer's body. Press the right foot hard on the floor and slide it backward, so as to cause the rubber band to roll off the shoe. This leaves the duplicate nine of hearts on the floor, a little in back of the mixed cards. While making the sliding motion with the right foot, bend downward and proceed to cover the cards with the paper. Great care must be taken in noting the exact position of the duplicate while the paper covers it. A picture on the newspaper is a good thing to lay directly over the card, so as to keep track of it. The performer now asks to be blindfolded, and also borrows a penknife. Magicians as a rule are aware of the fact that it is possible to see downward through a blindfold. Therefore it is a simple matter to plunge the knife through the newspaper at the point where the duplicate card lays, and bring the desired effect. ★

Location of slipped-off duplicate is memorized and ad or photo in paper is placed over it and pierced.

The performer claims an ability to spot the ace after it has been covered, along with other cards.

magical discovery

THIS IS ANOTHER excellent after-dinner effect, simple when explained, but mystifying while in presentation. The magician takes three cards—the ace, Jack and Queen of any suit—from a pack of cards and places them on a table. Three cardboard covers, a trifle longer and wider than the cards, are handed to some member of the gathering. He is instructed by the magician to shift the cards as he will and then cover them with the pieces of cardboard and he, the magician, will always pick out the ace. The magician leaves the room and the cards are moved around the table then covered with the cardboards. The magician returns, glances at the cardboard covers and every time picks out and turns over the ace card.

The simple explanation is this. The ace has a short hair pasted to it. No matter how it is moved around, the hair projects outside of the covers when cards are hidden from view. It is advisable to use a table cover of dark material so sharp eyes will not discover the *modus operandi*. ★

Performer leaves and returns, spots ace under the cover card; a short hair has been fastened to ace.